N. Bhaskara Rao is a pioneer of social research in India. He is Founder-Chairman of the Centre for Media Studies (CMS) and Marketing and Development Research Associates (MDRA). Earlier, he built up the equally prestigious Operations Research Group (ORG). He was a member, with Dr M.S. Swaminathan, of the high-level committee that drafted the National Population Policy, and an expert-member of the committee that reorganized the media units of the Information and Broadcasting Ministry. His books include *Social Impact of Mass Media* (1996), *A Handbook of Poll Surveys in Media* (2009), *The TRP Trick: How Television in India was Hijacked* (2019) and *The Third Eye of Governance: Rise of Populism, Decline in Social Research* (2021).

THE EMPEROR'S MIRROR

The State of Research in India

Dr N. Bhaskara Rao

SPEAKING TIGER

SPEAKING TIGER BOOKS LLP
125A, Ground Floor, Shahpur Jat, near Asiad Village,
New Delhi 110049

First published by Speaking Tiger Books in 2024

ISBN: 978-93-5447-771-3
eISBN: 978-93-5447-778-2

10 9 8 7 6 5 4 3 2 1

Typeset in Adobe Garamond Pro by SÜRYA, New Delhi
Printed at HT Media Ltd, Greater Noida

CONTENTS

PREFACE

Independent and transparent research is vital for good governance. It can even safeguard against bad governments. The status of independent research, assessment and evaluation of public policies signals that the governance, development and democracy of the country is on a safe course. Besides being a third eye of the government, reliable research is a barometer for the sustainability of development, harmony, prosperity and prospects of the people. This book attempts to track the turns that social and policy research has taken over the last 75 years. From a proactive position in the early decades of Independence, research has slipped to a new low in both role and status. If this trend is not reversed, research could become irrelevant and even dangerously misleading. Such a situation needs to be avoided. Independent research has suffered due to the preoccupation of different political regimes with polarisation and populism, and due to the egotism of leaders. But those in power and authority should realize the harm they do to the nation, to our democracy—and, indeed, to their own long-term prospects—by ignoring or wilfully rejecting the potential of independent research and reliable data in performance appraisal and effective governance.

India spends over Rs. 25 lac crore annually for socio-economic developmental endeavours. The Union Government alone spends Rs. 15 Lac crores annually on such 'developmental activities', covering over 700 schemes of Union Ministries. At least 10 per cent of the schemes should be research based. What has been the effort by the Government or others to look into the effectiveness, in terms of inclusivity, outcomes and course-correction, of these schemes? Do we spend even 0.01 per cent of that outlay for research and evaluation?

What is the standing and status of social research in India as a discipline, in application and in academia? How reliable and credible is its standing? What have the main concerns of research been? What is the research capability of the country? How independent are research agencies? (Not that an independent agency is necessarily independent in all its engagements.) Has there been a critical overview at any level of research and evaluation endeavours? In the case of social science research, for example, only three books in the last ten years can be said to have done credible work. The first two books, which have the same title, *Social Science Research in India*, were published in 2012 and 2017. Their review is limited to the working of the Indian Council of Social Science Research (ICSSR) and its affiliated agencies. The first book was edited by Dr M.V. Nadakarni and Dr R.S. Deshpande of the Institute for Social and Economic Change (ISEC). The second book was edited by Dr Sukhdeo Thorat and Samar Verma at the instance of ICSSR and was limited to a review of ICSSR's committees and their assessment of its operations. The third, an independent researcher's perspective, titled *The Third Eye of Governance: Rise of Populism, Decline in Social*

Research was my own, published in 2021. That is all. And there has been no professional review of any kind whatsoever of over a dozen tribal research centres nor of the several population research centres which have been in existence for decades. In fact, many—even ICSSR-recognised—research agencies, in existence for fifty years, are in the wilderness today.

Unlike in scientific research, the findings of policy/social research can be short lived. They may be topical, riddled with intrigues and soon forgotten, or even ignored for different reasons. But when the research is independent, transparent and without conflict of interest, the institute may survive longer, gain repute and may even further the research potential. Applied social science research is multidisciplinary. The more the disciplines involved, the greater and wider the relevance of the research, as each discipline offers its own perspective and inclusive methodology.

Most scientific research is by institutions with proper credentials, but this is not always so in the case of public research. Most social science research is academic, and policy research remains within the orbit of the Government. Since independent research often lays bare the activities of the establishment, it is often not supported. As our leaders focus on their own perceptions, image and influence have become the priority, and as a result, the velocity of research has declined. This is evident in the curtailed support for social research in recent years. And there are always those who differ or question or even oppose the findings of research. No research is value free. But by being transparent and self-appraising, research acquires credibility. The belief that research has a public service slant or 'Socratic concern' could be a safeguard against its decline.

In the last decade, no new research resource, independent or otherwise, has come up in the country. Now, unusually, even the decadal 2021 Census is being deferred as never before, and even the only authentic data on births and deaths for the country was stopped in 2021-22. Research is now more a matter of rhetoric. Budget and actual allocation for research continue to decline. Why should the authorities interrupt or avoid putting out basic primary data on public services as in the case of child labour, farmer suicides, manual scavenging, and poverty levels, for example? The research institutes which remain somewhat active are the ones which operate in service of the powers. No independent research agency could last today without depending on foreign or corporate support. Hardly any provision for social responsibility concerns is evident. As independent research based think-tanks, institutions like CSD, CSDS, CSE, CPR, PAC and CMS offer a model for upholding the potential of this 'third eye' of governance. More recently a couple of universities, like Ashoka, too have acquired standing.

The agencies that have withered away as independent research outfits were the ones that relied on external support, or government funding, or ended up spending over 25 per cent of turnover on overheads or over fifty per cent on establishment (salaries). Economic viability is as important and perhaps even more critical than societal relevance, independence and transparency. It is important to understand how different independent institutes survived through changing political regimes. How successive governments availed of or ignored independent agencies' feedback, monitoring, research and evaluation is also significant. As Dr R.A. Mashelkar observed in his foreword to *Third Eye*, 'We must succeed in this so that public policy research can assume its rightful and powerful role as the Third Eye of Governance'.

In the writing of this book, I have had perhaps as many limitations as advantages. During my 55 years as an 'activist researcher', there were situations which led me to find ways without compromising the core values of research. The idea of CMS is 50 years old. Its unique 35-year saga as an independent institution has seen many innovations and examples for proactive initiatives. A closer look at CMS's journey reveals the opportunities both missed and utilised.

I specially thank Dr Rajiv Kumar, former Vice Chair of NITI Aayog, for his suggestions.

Dr N. Bhaskara Rao

1

RESEARCH IS AN OPPORTUNITY, NOT A DILEMMA

Wither Research? A Dilemma

In years past, India was known more for its population size, poverty and illiteracy. But now, 75 years after independence, India is viewed as a powerhouse for its contributions to scientific, technological, managerial and economic matters. Even in entrepreneurship and wealth creation, India is among the leading nations of the world. Many nations, big and small, democratic or otherwise, are looking towards India for new directions. More than 3.5 crore people of Indian origin are active in whichever country they are, in whatever capacity; they have earned honour for themselves and the country. Its inherent strengths allowed India to defy doubters who prophesied that India would not survive as a united country.

Seventy years ago India witnessed one crisis after another, starting with floods and droughts, followed by food shortages and this made it desperate to import food grains. Today, farmers want to export rice, wheat and fruit, etc. Today

India exports lifesaving drugs to many countries and has even been described as the pharmacy of the world. The average age in India in 2022 was above 65 years, compared to less than 30 years merely 80 years ago. While we continue to import defence equipment (for old systems) India today exports satellites as well as defence equipment. Not only did we safeguard our independence, India has been successful in increasing its role globally. In a world shaped by the collapse of the Soviet Union and spread of globalisation, India has leveraged her growing capabilities.

The foundations laid in the first two decades of India's independence were unparalleled among the new democracies. The urge for a national and scientific base was unprecedented and the research spirit evident among leaders. The recent Mangalyaan project, or GSAT, are examples of such a spirit. Disciplines such as science, technology and management were fostered, and institutions such as ISRO were established. The growth of these institutions, their earnestness and professionalism enriched the country's research orientation. All this has driven India today to the top of the world in terms of innovation, technology and scientific outlook and in tackling the socio-economic issues confronting the country.

This did not happen overnight or in a decade or in one term of a government. Successive governments took insights from elders of previous decades and contributed their own ideas. Despite instances of complacency of some leaders or changes in priorities, we have not remained 'under developed' as the UN agencies described until a few years ago. Every five years, over 5000 elected leaders to legislatures and 32 lacs to local panchayats, have played their role in developing the country to its present level. Over the course of 17 general elections, 12 times the incumbent was changed or a different political party or combination, including ideologically opposing ones, came to power, peacefully. All of the nation's accomplishments have been against the backdrop of our political system with its representative form of government and rule of law, unlike the China model where individual rights were never allowed, or even the two party system of democracy of the UK. Authoritarian rule in China may have given it an advantage for various reasons. But it was research which enabled India to overcome difficulties and consolidate as a nation. It was the planning approach, strategic interventions backed by data, a futuristic outlook and visionary leaders which took India to new heights and gave it a distinct stature. The emphasis on planning and research in the early years of Independence helped India solve some of her problems as well as gear up for the future.

Trends in MMR in India

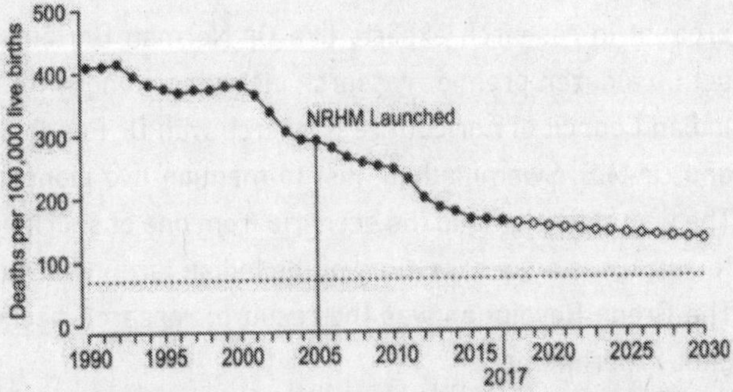

Source: Adapted by author from Vos et al. 2017 and additional data accessed from The Global Burden of Disease study (provided by the Institute of Health Metrics and Evaluation).

(Dr Srikanth Reddy, 2019 Make Health in India. Rural Health Mission)

Many examples can be cited for how research helped the country, through a 'take the bull by the horns' approach. That approach allowed India to perhaps accomplish more in the initial two decades than what it did in the later four decades. Research has helped avert massive malnutrition and communicable diseases like Cholera and TB. Research helped India shake off the pessimist forecasts about the new republic. Below are three examples to remind us about how that transition took place.

Research As a Catalyst

One classic example of the role of research as a catalyst was in addressing food shortages and the farming crisis. The high number of agricultural colleges, demonstration centres and a policy approach based on extensive research conducted across the country helped overcome the crisis much faster. The Indian Agriculture Research Institute emerged as the nucleus. The Rockefeller Foundation brought in research experts like Dr Norman Borlaug to set up a dozen premier research institutes along with the Indian Council of Agriculture Research with Dr Randhawa and Dr M.S. Swaminathan, just to mention two pioneers. The way India changed the scenario from one of shortages to surplus is a success story of the Indian farming sector. The Green Revolution was the result of research-backed pilot experiments.

Another example is the way population growth was addressed. The visionaries of the time quickly realised that without addressing population growth, development and equity would be difficult. Early research within the country included the Hooghly Study on 'social marketing', the Kapurthala study on 'cafeteria approach' and the insights from demographic research centres which experts like Dr Ashish Bose had put together to bring out the challenge faced by BIMARU states. In 1970, the first National Study on Family Planning Practices of ORG (financed by the Ford Foundation and the Ministry of Health and Family Planning) helped integrate research into the national policy framework. These studies helped change the prevalent attitudes towards family size from 'the more, the merrier', and the preference for sons to the '*hum do, hamare do*' view. Even J.R.D. Tata funded and set up population research initiatives. All this took place in 20 years (1965-85).

Rural development was yet another distinct initiative based on research insights and field research like that from Nilokheri in Haryana and Etawah in Uttar Pradesh. The approach of community development based on extension, education and field visits was taken up vigorously. The Balwantrai Mehta Report on decentralised development, using a participative approach, recognised various pilot projects which were then scaled up. These research efforts helped to expedite development in different regions of the country. The National Institute of Rural Development and Rural Electricity Corporation were set up. Research on these experiments and pilots helped India come up with new initiatives.

> There are many other examples to bring out the role of research. I give these three examples because I myself was associated with them from 1962 to 1985. I was part of the campaign for nitrogen fertiliser promotion, and I was associated with *'do ya teen'* and similar campaigns based on the report I wrote on the first national survey on family planning practices (1972).

Many distinct factors contributed to what we have accomplished, overcoming multiple stumbling blocks. In my view, these include the following. The first is the focus with which serious concerns were taken up. Second, the foregrounding of science and a rational approach. Third, the fact that our political system facilitated the involvement and participation of many people. Fourth, the institutional approach which ensured continuity, relevance and independence. Fifth, data-based planning, decisions and implementation. Sixth, the decentralised nature of governance and responsibilities, and respecting constitutional obligations like holding elections regularly, and adhering to checks and balances.

Today we also stand out as an example globally for creative talent to reap the potential of newer technologies. All this was possible despite the divides of caste, multiplicity of political parties and the vagaries of Nature. Research on socio-economic demographics and different educational priorities has allowed India to participate on the global stage. But there is another side which cannot be ignored. It can be said that we have not taken seriously to critical research, or engaged with futures studies and decentralised implementation.

Are Global Indexes Unfair to India?

Much research on India and the lives of Indians and their potential has been carried out outside India. German scholars were among the first to study Indian society and belief systems. In the early 1960s, ten American Universities set up 'India centres'. They acquired every book published in India and Indian research and became repositories of knowledge on India in the US. This enabled American faculties to undertake research and analysis on India even before Indian academics were ready to do so. Myron Weiner, Paul Brass and Susanne Rudolf are examples of those early pioneers of research on India.

This kind of research at different universities, by different faculties on a range of themes, gave US academics a certain advantage in terms of analytical argument on India. The American State Department availed of this expertise. John Foster Dulles, Secretary of State (1953-59) gave a push to this 'search India' research by US scholars. This encouragement led some faculties to start initiatives like the 'Global Index'. After the 1970s it was former World Bank consultants who took up the ranking of countries as to quantify the trajectory of development, democracy and governance.

In recent years, India has been ranked low year after year in many Global Indexes including by academics in the US, Germany, Sweden, etc. They try to substantiate their ratings with methodologies and sources of data. Not all of them, however, are transparent. Many of them have engaged in such exercises for years. Initially, the Indian Government ignored the ratings. Later, it tried to (allegedly) influence the agencies to adjust or change the rankings favourably, instead of providing a plausible explanation. This explanation could involve the definition of concepts, sources of data and validation of the data concerned. These Global Indexes have not reported any prior discussions with concerned Indian authorities or Indian experts outside the country.

In the last couple of years, the Indian Government (through the NITI Aayog) has taken to performance assessment on a number of issues using the 'global index model' for ranking and rating the states and public services within the country.

In July 2022 the Government of India rejected the 2022 Environmental Performance Index, saying that 'it makes use of biased metrics and weights' on air quality and rapidly increasing greenhouse gases. This was not the first time the Government reacted this way on the Environment Performance ranking. Its behaviour has been similar over India's ranking in some other areas like democracy and freedom. Interestingly, in July 2022, the Government claimed that the Environment Global Index emphasised the 'extent' of protected area, rather than the 'quality' of protection. Year after year, the ranking was rebutted on the grounds that 'Management Effectiveness Evaluation of protected area is not factored in the computation.' The core of the issue underlying the Index, or the context, was overlooked.

The reaction of the Government to the 2022 Global Index on Hunger was similar. The impression the Index gives is that Indian children go hungry and are among the most neglected despite the initiatives over the decades, which have been both specific and massive in terms of focus and outlay. But, at the same time, the Prime Minister has cited global indexes whenever it has suited the government, when they reflect some improvement, as for example in 2019 and again in November 2022 on the topic of Innovations, thereby giving legitimacy to Global Indexes.

Why does such a situation continue? It is not that only Global Indexes have been rating India low on critical rankings year after year. The claims made by the government are not in sync with global ratings.

But then it is not only Global Indexes which present India's performance as far below average. There are many voices, political and professional, within the country too who are critical of and who contest the claims of leaders of the government. In fact, these domestic voices are even more critical and specific. For example, on Democracy, Press Freedom, Environmental Performance, multiple Global Indexes and voices at home bring out the fact that something is missing in India's story of development and accomplishments. The Government is either not able to put forward the 'achievement' claims convincingly or in the right context, or it exaggerates the accomplishment, unconcerned or disconnected with the ground realities. In all these instances, what is missing is independent researchers, a conducive research milieu and credible voices. The data sources, assessment, analysis and evaluation and their credibility are either doubtworthy or inconsistent or not substantiated. This lack of reliable data has allowed a contentious atmosphere to develop, as the performance indicated or claimed cannot not be validated. There is no independent voice of individuals or institutes, and successive governments have not addressed this lack with the kind of seriousness that it requires. But how can this be, year after year, and lasting beyond a decade? As if India has not changed over these years or is unconcerned with even dispassionate criticism of its course?

The research, that is the data, analysis and findings compiled by the government itself is not taken at face value. Most of it is presumed exaggerated to suit the government of the day or by sources responsible for implementation without independent validation. This is in contrast to India's background as the country of pioneers in the field of statistics, analytical expertise and research agencies which have been engaged in monitoring, accumulating data and compiling indexes professionally to a high standard. Our research agencies have impressive infrastructure, backed by subject experts and years of research insights. And yet research experts are not involved prominently in the research endeavours of the government.

Reliable research would save India from the rankings and ratings that we see in global indexes and ensure that the performance on the ground is corrected or improved. Research includes data, field facts, analysis of data, understanding the linkages between variables, impact and evaluation, estimations and report preparation. It also involves advocating for justifying the indices and concepts involved in the processes of global ranking.

The research infrastructure and capabilities in the country have been acknowledged the world over in the last couple of decades and, in fact, statistical and computer science academia in the US, for example, has been bolstered by Indian-origin scholars for some years. Even in India, in the earlier decades after Independence, research had made impressive contributions, though this was never acknowledged. And yet today, research neither seems to make a difference at home nor help in tackling the dilemma arising out Global Indexes or critics within the country.

The impression one gets is that we have begun to disregard serious, independent research even where it is much needed. It is becoming increasingly evident that it is election time promises and the claims of leaders that drive data and research. This leads to a temporary outlook and limits the tune and scope of research. Politicians the world over do not feel comfortable with independent research. Those in power would rather have 'supportive' data or 'endorsement research'.

Lately, there have been no data claims on public issues by responsible government institutions, the Right to Information Act has been undermined, and apex level judicial regulations have been ignored, and this signals an impending credibility crisis of not just the government but the country's standing on the whole. It is also a failure of the 'checks and balance' provisions of the Indian state.

A Data Protection Bill under consideration in early 2023 by Parliament quietly proposes in section 30(2) to amend section 8(1)(J) of the Right to Information Act and thereby vitiate the very provisions of the RTI Act. It further shuts down transparency in research and data, as the very credibility of data will be under threat.

There has not been an appraisal of research capabilities and their utilisation in fulfilling the primary objectives as indicated in the Constitution, of what the Republic is expected to accomplish. The research efforts of academics have not been looked into. Despite the country's 'New India' development direction, not a single Indian research institute has been globally recognised in the social or development sector. An effort is made in this book, using a couple of examples, to explain where and why we are unable to benefit from research. The scope of research, its challenges and opportunities today are different from the previous decades.

The New Education Policy of 2020, for example, has provided proposals to revive the research apparatus and its utilisation in the country. But there has been no discussion of the implications of proposals like constituting a Research Foundation headed by the Prime Minister. The policy also implies that no distinction exists between social science research and research in the physical sciences and technology.

Rainbow View of Policy Research

Government sponsorship of research on contentious issues tends to promote a distorted picture and dampens the credibility of the research itself. There is no visibility of independent research in the country, despite the existence of independent research institutes and agencies. The news media also tends to ignore or underplay independent research because of certain perceptions about authenticity and overplays research endorsed by the government. This is a misconception: independent research is not anti-government. In fact, independent research could be a more credible supporter of the government, both directly and indirectly.

What India needs today is a framework to take advantage of independent research in the interests of development, democracy and governance. Successive governments have not realised the significance and relevance of independent research.

This however does not mean that we do not have the

expertise or capability to offer the country a specific, utilitarian approach. In fact, it was our own Dr P.C. Mahalanobis who, on invitation from the UN more than seventy years ago, had set up the global statistical measurements framework. Ever since, most US premier universities' statistics, computer science and information technology departments are led by those from Indian Institutes.

Over the past few years, we have either lost our initiative or derailed our own capabilities, and demoralised our independent professionals and institutions with credentials both at home and abroad. This distortion cannot be corrected overnight or in one five-year term of a Prime Minister. This is not a matter of one institute or department or leader in isolation. Research credibility does not come from one piece of critical research. Fundamental research has to be an ongoing, ingrained pursuit.

Half a dozen Indian research outfits were taken over by a foreign or multinational research agency in the wake of economic reforms in the 1990s, and more than a dozen foreign research agencies entered the field, playing an active role and enjoying a certain preferential treatment. ORG, MARG, MRAS, MODE, among others, were the prominent Indian agencies which disappeared. EY, Deloitte, TNS, Kantar, AC Neilson, IPSOS, KPMG, Frost, Research Pacific, Gartner, Millward Brown, Oxford, were among the foreign agencies entering the country, engaging in market, social and economic research in India. No Indian professional is at the helm of affairs or in senior positions in any of these foreign research agencies who are engaged in analysing wide ranging data.

Early Origins of Social Research

The discipline of social science research and applied social research has its origins in the Second World War and in post-war campaigns, from 1935-50. The main concern can be said to be propaganda and influence. The research of Harold Lasswell and Paul Lazarsfeld, American social scientists, is legendary. The initial impetus for their research was war time communication. The next phase (1950-75) was concerned with productivity and motivation. The main thrust of research was awareness, aspirations and motivation. Apart from academics, economic bodies like the IMF and the World Bank became involved in research on economics and investments. Simultaneously, aid agencies like US AID, the Rockefeller Foundation, and the Ford Foundation became interested in entering countries under different stages of development, providing external guidance and aid. In the process, some of the existing criteria and models of those countries like the USA and UK were introduced to other countries and adopted for research as well as for 'development'. Indian leaders who were anxious to seek assistance in their endeavours to overcome the era of shortages, followed some of the same research methodologies.

By the 1950s, the International Monitory Fund (IMF), the World Bank, and the UN and its agencies like UNDP, UNICEF, WHO and UNESCO emerged as proponents of models for growth and development with their research-based consultations. The USA and UK as well as Germany, France and USSR had also stepped into the aid arena, each with their own priorities, and in the process promoted their 'market models' to the extent that countries like India were tempted to adopt these models without assessing the local relevance of those models, and even without consultations within the country.

That was how a 'top down' approach became the dominant development model. That was also when 'development research' became a specialised form of research, sought by the government, public services, aid agencies, international bodies and even by civil society organisations.

Then came the phase when people's participation in the implementation of developmental programmes began to drive research, but this kind of research was mostly by a few independent scholars whose motivation was not always known. Most often they were academics or driven by activism.

But, since 1995, the main concern of research has been wooing voters and image building, driven by publicity and propaganda. That is when the priority shifted from implementation to information and image building, and from citizen to voter. In this shift, the use of information and the implications of research have become a secondary concern. Instead, public relations has become the priority. In this process, particularly since 2015, fake, planted and surrogate news coverage has become a research concern. Proliferation of new digital tools has facilitated this shift in priority. 'Quid pro quo' communication instead of motivational research has become a priority. Perceptions, rather than experience, have become the main concern of research methodologies.

It is rather disappointing that despite social research in India being more than fifty years old, it cannot claim a foundation of India-centric fundamentals. Nor do any compatible baselines or benchmarks exist on vital data parameters to do with development, public policies, social change, life styles and governance specific to India. Social research seems to have lost its way despite several initiatives as a part of a quest for scientific temper that the first Prime Minister of India had spearheaded. In my analysis, social science research is a missing link in India's development growth pursuit. How did this happen?

Declining Support for Policy Research

How much do governments spend on research and evaluation? Obviously, this figure will reflect the level of importance that a country gives to research. It was insignificant according an estimate of mine some years ago, when it was hardly 0.3 per cent of project/scheme budgets. More recently in 2017-18, I estimated that what was spent by the Union Government and the state governments for research was hardly 1.0 per cent of the budgets for various development and welfare schemes. A rough estimate indicates that not even half of what is budgeted and allocated is actually disbursed. And, what is spent is less than one-third of the amount spent on advertising and publicity for government schemes, which I estimated in 2020 at around Rs. 20,000 crores yearly (for 2016-18). What was being actually spent on all kind of research, monitoring and evaluation activities of the social sector by various governments (at Union and State level) and their departments was around Rs.7000 crores annually (in 2014-15).

What the UGC (University Grants Commission) and ICSSR spends on research is an indicator of the significance the country gives to research culture. While the UGC nurtures academics, ICSSR promotes practice and the profession. A critical review of what these driving agencies spend brings out, glaringly, the importance research is given in the country. For example, the ICSSR annual budget, including support to 27 research institutes, was hardly Rs. 100 crores in 2010 (in 2020 it was around Rs. 200 crores). What is even more alarming is that only one third of that was actually spent on research, the rest was for establishment and administrative costs. The amount allocated by the UGC for social science research has been declining for two decades. And of what is shown as allocated, not even half is actually spent. This has been the case for several years, as indicated by the table below. In 2022, Dr Narayana Murthy of Infosys reminded the country that, 'investment into research is unsatisfactory', with 'insufficient' grants and an 'inability to use research'.

Is the decline deliberate? It is noteworthy that this reduction took place at a time when the national budgets were increased significantly and the number of schemes and initiatives of the government multiplied and were launched nationally simultaneously, which requires considerable research support and backup initially and for monitoring and evaluation.

A former UGC secretary, R.K. Chauhan, confirmed that 'the Government had reduced funding for the UGC which is why research was getting least priority. As a result, UGC has no funds for research, particularly in social science and humanities. It fears that the findings will not suit its narratives.' Chauhan said that this is because such research typically looks into the state of employment in the country. Chauhan narrated how the decline in funding was affecting the research environment in universities. This is echoed by Prof. Mohan Kumar of Kerala University, who says that, 'Indian Universities are largely lagging behind those in advanced countries.'

The news media had prominently reported that the UGC had stopped research projects due to lack of funds from the Union Government. The annual reports of the UGC and its website and data presented in the Parliament in February 2022 confirm that for the past five years funding for research schemes has been declining and in some cases projects were declared closed. UGC hardly spends 15 per cent of its budget for research in social science and basic science. The total grants to ICSSR are hardly 10 per cent of what CSIR (Council of Scientific and Industrial Research) is allotted.

The decline did not start in 2014 but much before; however, it has been accelerating over the last decade, as shown by these tables. The story of ICSSR is enough to expose this trend. There is also the example of TIFAC (which is concerned with technology forecasting) which had Dr Abdul Kalam as Chair and Dr Y.S. Rajan as executive director, which was expected to unleash forecasting research 40 years ago. It has been brought under the care of the DST (Department of Science & Technology) and is now devoted more to conferences and consultations, after initiating a good number of research studies.

UGC Funds for Social Science: Allocated and Released

Year	UGC Grants to Social Science Research Allocation (in Crore)	Funds Released to Universities (in Crore)
2008-09	71.03	28
2009-10	89.21	20.7
2010-11	84.61	24.3
2011-12	51.21	11.2
2012-13	74.09	47.5
2013-14	39.06	(stopped giving)
2016-17	26.26	Not available
2017-18	23.58	Not available
2018-19	11.45	Not available
2019-20	3.27	Not available
2020-21	0.38	Not available

Source: Sukhadeo Thorat and Samar Verma, *Social Science Research* in India, 2017

Union Ministries annually receive around Rs. 1000 crores for social science research. How much of that is spent for actual research can only be a guessed estimate in the absence of any official accounts or budgetary figures.

Number of Research Scholars with UGC Support

Year	Number of Research Scholars
2015-16	2900
2016-17	1200
2017-18	1422
2018-19	1088
2019-20	335

Source: UGC

In the Union Budget for 2022, funds for the schemes were cut to 17.26 crore from Rs. 25 crores in 2021-22. The actual expenditure was only around 12 crores. Funds for the Maulana Azad Education Foundation, for example, were cut from 70 crores in 2019-20 to one lac in 2022.

Awards, rewards and similar incentives help consolidate the gains in professional institutes, and build up standards in the pursuit of research. Individual incentives go a long way in promoting a research culture. On September 9, 2022, while inaugurating the Centre-State Science Technology Conference at Ahmedabad, Prime Minister Modi claimed that 'it is because of recent initiatives that India's rank in "Global innovation Index" has gone up from 81 in 2015 to 40 in 2022.' He rightly suggested that India should be a global centre for 'research and innovation'. But within a fortnight after that, the government announced the cancellation of annual awards for scientific research which had been given to scientific and medical researchers for some years. Over 300 awards, including National Awards, are given by various departments and Ministries like the Department of Science and Technology, the Department of Biotechnology, Ministry of Earth Sciences, CSIR, the Department of Atomic Energy, and the Indian Council of Medical Research. Nearly half of these awards were instituted by private endowments and many awards carry scholarships and fellowships. The only explanation given for the cancellation of these awards was 'to start a new scheme with full justification and detailed guidelines' and to award 'really deserving candidates'. One can imagine what message this sends and how such a devastating decision would be viewed by the research institutes, academics and research community across the country.

In Delhi, a premier national institute, the All India Institute of Medical Science (AIIMS) was ordered in October 2022 not to invite any prominent personalities to its campus, including to research faculties, without the permission of the

Minister who happened to be the chair of the autonomous body. Such directives highlight the vulnerability of research institutes and their research priorities.

In 2018, when the HRD Ministry issued a directive to the vice chancellors and directors of national institutes that PhD theses should not be on 'irrelevant topics' and should be on subjects of 'national priorities', there was widespread concern. Such decisions obviously cause concern and raise doubts about the intentions of the authorities, which in turn impacts how official data and assessments are viewed.

In response to a US submission to the WTO in 2019, India submitted that it was a 'developing country' with not only a very low per capita income but also a 'very low research and development capacity'. Through this response of the Indian government, India missed an opportunity to position itself on the global scene as 'New India'.

India has come a long way on its growth path. It has accomplished much, and overcome early calamities and crises by availing of planning and research and taking a rational approach. The credit for that goes not to any one regime or government, but to the contribution of a number of leaders from the bottom up in 17 general elections. What was achieved in the first 20 years was far more than the next 40 years. One factor in this decline is that research, which played an active role in the initial decades, has been denigrated or downplayed, coinciding with the rise of political parties and their leaders' desire for popularity. The governments of late have not been serious about research. Budgets have been curtailed. The expectations of research have been that it should be supportive or endorsing. Research's third eye potential is being missed. It has been reduced to 'rainbow status'; that is, the research findings are ephemeral, and soon forgotten.

This decline in the stature of social research in the country signals a decline in policy formulation and in the implementation of massive public schemes. The decline of research in India has been pointed out over the last 20 years by independent professionals. Professor P. Chatterjee identified this trend in 2002 in his article in the *Economic and Political Weekly* (EPW). It was reiterated by the International Development Research Centre (IDRC) in 2008 in a round table meet of experts, held as a follow up to an early alarm in 2007 by the ICSSR itself in its review report. Professor T.S. Papola in 2010 elaborated the trend in an Institute for Studies in Industrial Development (ISID) paper. It was reiterated by the UK government's Department for International Development in its 'Mapping Report' in 2011 on 'Social Science Research in India'. Even the ICSSR had three reviews by eminent independent experts in the last 30 years with no cognizance and follow up. Nothing has changed, no effort is evident at any level to reverse the trend.

Several critical lacunae have been pointed out as responsible for the decline of research. These include a lack of review of the quality of research; the slashing of budgets for research; the lack of institutional approach and support; the lack of support to research in the universities; and the fact that research is not being used in policy formulation, nor is research entering the public domain with any transparency. A concern was also expressed about the increasing negative influence of foreign donor agencies sponsoring or commissioning research.

As if to confirm the unconcern of the government towards

primary data, the government has deferred the 2021 census operations. As of January 2023 there was no indication when this two-phased exercise, involving more than a million enumerators, would commence. Every decade, the Census operation requires rigorous research instruments and consultations both politically and professionally. There is no indication of the transparency necessary for the credibility of such vital primary data, as if the government does not want a trend analysis and does not care about the implications of this deferral of the 2021 Census operations for the country's research credibility.

India today is in a better position in many respects. Globally Indians, not just the technocrats, are valued far more than ever before. Prime Minister Narendra Modi, who has helped build that momentum, has the best opportunity now to bring much needed credibility to data and research in general and particularly of the government. Going by the rankings of 33 global indexes in 2022-23, India's claims and data are not taken at face value internationally. Only when we change this standing by restoring the credibility of our statistics and research, will India be viewed as 'developed' instead of continuing to be described as a 'developing' country. Only then can its governments claim to be giving 'good governance' to the people.

2

DEVELOPMENT, BUT NOT WITHOUT RESEARCH

Beginnings of a Planned, Independent India

India was blessed, 50 years before it became a free country, with a series of visionary leaders who articulated how India should develop when it became independent. Great minds contributed to India's awakening, its preparedness and process of becoming a nation of substance. From the 1920s onwards, leaders like Gopal Krishna Gokhale, Dadabhai Naoroji, Bal Gangadhar Tilak, Pherozeshah Mehta, Lala Lajpat Rai, Chittaranjan Das, P.D. Tandon, C. Rajagopalachari, Subhas Chandra Bose and Jawaharlal Nehru, to mention a few, advocated a Swadeshi model. Mahatma Gandhi's contribution was unparalleled. Gandhi cautioned against the fate of India if it aped the West, and that it was 'impossible for India today to become England'. He advised the country not to adopt the same 'resource intense society'. Even after his death, Gandhi's idea of a self-reliant India was upheld.

In 1937, Subhas Chandra Bose and Meghnad Saha came

up with the idea of a commission to address the issue of India becoming an independent nation. In his address to the Hapur AIC Congress in 1938, Bose suggested a strategy for socio economic development and reconstruction. He even pointed out that extensive surveys and collection of data would be essential. Meghnad Saha, a foremost scientist, mooted the idea of establishing a national research council and mobilising the 'scientific intelligence of the country'. It was Saha who invited Subhas Chandra Bose to the India Science Association.

Those foundational years provided guiding insights worth remembering. These included acceptance of different points of view, plurality in thinking and promoting equality of opportunities. Respect for dissent was a cherished value. For the nation's early leaders, there were 'no rivals, only colleagues,' and vengeance was never part of the discourse. Tolerance and respect remained a hallmark of that generation of leaders. 'Unity in diversity' was a reality, not merely a credo.

Differences were viewed as strength, not weakness, and even dissent was welcomed. PM Jawaharlal Nehru allowed and encouraged, as chief of the ruling party, a dissenting group of MPs and leaders to articulate their views openly, and welcomed critical press.

Jawaharlal Nehru named his famous book *Discovery of India* (*Bharat Ek Khoj*), written from various prisons during 1942-46. It was based on the Upanishads, Vedas and the history of ancient India. It reminds readers of the broad base of Indian philosophy, culture and governance. Most of the leaders of the time cautioned against India adopting Western models of development. After becoming Prime Minister, however, I feel that Nehru took a different path from the one described in his own book.

Before the concept of 'development' came into vogue, the ideals of harmony, happiness, wisdom, sharing and conservation, were the main concerns of our early leaders. These are mostly qualitative ideals. The desire was to foster a cooperative and collaborative outlook in the people, rather than the idea of competition and the rat race of the West.

Had we stuck to this approach to development, perhaps the global agencies would not have judged India on how well it aped the lifestyle of Western countries, or used Western-centric criteria or indicators for development and economic growth.

It was the 1931 Census which first categorised certain castes and communities as 'depressed classes'. Based on that data the Government of India Act 1935 notified the 'socially disadvantaged' as coming under 'scheduled castes'. Thereafter, when the Indian Constitution abolished untouchability in 1950, it provided for several 'special safe-guards' for attaining equality. The eligibility criteria for all these categories was based on numbers, and this led to the rise of data gathering and field surveys. The desire to protect vulnerable groups, which required them to first be identified, highlighted the relevance of data from the field and analyses of the same. This was the basis for the inclusive social justice policies of successive governments, which after 1980 become politicised, which meant that their implementation depended upon which party or leader was in power.

Somewhere along the line after the first 20 years of independence, UN organisations and the World Bank, the IMF and other global agencies went from advising to suggesting and then prescribing criteria for 'developing countries' and monitoring their implementation. We seem have fallen prey to alien ideas in the absence of articulation and advocacy of our own, time-tested ideas on development, tranquillity, happiness, etc. Even now despite having the talent and infrastructure, India has not put forward a distinct model of development with criteria for change or performance. Such a model would not necessarily be an alternative model of development to that of the West but an exercise in nurturing our own time-tested values, beliefs, our future-oriented and Nature-preserving culture. In the name of 'modernity' we have de-rooted ourselves from that 'traditional course'. How could anything be considered 'development' without social justice, equal opportunities, harmony and happiness and a collaborative outlook? Where Nature is not respected and preserved?

None of the prescriptions of any of the global agencies, including the UNDP and World Bank, have made much difference over the years on most of their own development indicators. This includes economic and social development and consolidating the federal structure of the Indian republic. The UN pursued its SDG (Sustainable Development Goals) formula and then after failing to make much difference, pushed SDG-II with a deadline of 2018-19 and now 2030. Whatever difference has been made, it is selective, isolated and not sustainable. Our own pioneers, like Dr M.S. Swaminathan, for example, have been arguing for 'sustainable development' for decades but the Government has been more interested in global agencies' models, which are mostly quantitative, as if unconcerned about true sustainability.

The UN made it obligatory for countries to push the monitoring and evaluation of SDGs, particularly in India. And yet there is no evidence of any difference on any of the indicators. It is obvious that global politics has played a role in legitimising policies which benefit the rich. The research paradigm used to assess the SDGs is Western, as are initiatives to assess the difference various schemes have made to any section of population. Development has been taken over by politics.

Two trends have been alarming over these decades. First, economic inequalities have increased and the gap between rich and poor has not narrowed. The second trend, which has received a boost in recent years, is the dependency of citizens, the vulnerable and women in particular, on the government in the name of welfare and development.

An example from my own village demonstrates the misguided direction of development policies. There is an increasing trend for some children in Andhra Pradesh to claim that they don't know Telugu, their local language, as if studying in English in itself signifies 'development' or 'modernity'. No development can be sustainable if the criteria for assessing it are based on increasing spending and consuming. That is what we have ended up with. The UN's Index on human development considers that 'people and their capabilities to spend should be the ultimate criteria for assessing the development of a country, not economic growth alone.'

I was personally involved with three instances, which are mentioned here as examples of how criteria for development are misplaced. The first was during 1970-80 when UNESCO suggested to countries what it considered the right criteria for development. One of its suggestions was that countries should have 100 copies of a newspaper per 1000 people, working out to roughly one newspaper for every 10 as a precondition for considering a country as developed. This suggestion ignored the redundancy of having so many copies. Each country has their own culture of sharing news and the fact that a copy in India was read by more than ten people on an average was ignored (in 1970-72). Even more importantly, UNESCO ignored what that prescription meant for a country's forests and environment. To have newsprint for newspapers, trees must be cut. In August 1970, I went to UNESCO to put forward this point and in 1974-75 spoke with the Minister for Information & Broadcasting (I.K. Gujral) who was also the Urban Development Minister who had received the letter from UNESCO to consider their proposal.

My second example shows again how global agencies use definitions and concepts uniformly across diverse countries. The World Bank conducts a periodical 'cost of living index survey' in a couple of continents. This Index is the basis for the World Bank's lending policies and support to countries for their development programmes. India was part of a three-country study in 1979-80. The Indian Statistical Institute was a collaborator of this study in India with the World Bank. It took the Operation Research Group's help to actually conduct the field work, for which I was the coordinator from ORG. The questionnaire used for this study, sent by the World Bank, included criteria like 'shoe being used, amount of rice consumed, newspaper subscribed to, kind of transport used' and the like. I questioned the relevance of such criteria in the Indian context. After prolonged discussion and reluctance, such irrelevant questions were modified. This was possible then because the argument was made by an independent, credible and experienced survey research agency of India.

A third example involves the structure of houses considered necessary for development. Why should a concrete roof be the requirement of a 'liveable house'? Houses made with local material, which is more adaptable to local climate and seasons and also helps sustain the local economy, are ignored in preference for cement and steel based houses, with materials brought from outside. That a local model house is durable for longer than 20 years and works out to only 10-15 per cent of the cost of the type of concrete houses being promoted by the government was ignored, making the rural poor further impoverished and debt-prone.

Further, certain statistics in the Census have mislead India into adopting a development model which is alien to India's culture and climate. Three other examples given here should clarify the kind of distortion brought about by the development paradigm. For example, the idea of a 'Pucca' house as in the biannual Census questionnaire and report is interpreted to mean that those who do not have a 'Pucca' house with a concrete roof are poor, 'under developed' and need to be assisted with building a 'Pucca' house with non-local material. This innocuous statistic in the Census was never looked into or reviewed for its implications. The structure of housing, and the way governments went about constructing lacs of concrete houses with all building material (cement, concrete, sand, steel, etc.) brought from outside has made villages more debt-ridden and destabilised local economies.

For example, a house made with locally available material is not even eligible for a bank loan. Any research undertaken to measure development has accepted this distorted view on housing.

A second example was what the Census showed as the percentage of women in the work force. The 1941, 1951 and even 1961 Census reports showed the number of 'working' women as far below their actual role in productivity, economy and living. This deprived women of their due priority and share in resource allocation and development planning. As a result, we have lagged behind in terms of social development and many regions continue to languish. Very little research has highlighted this distortion. ORG demonstrated, with field surveys in collaboration with the Census organisation itself, how participation of women in the 'labour force' was significantly higher than what successive governments and research studies had considered.

A third example, the number of psychiatrists per 1000, which is taken as a criteria for development by the World Bank, is irrelevant for India in terms of global ranking. Family ties are strong in India; parents, siblings, even neighbours matter a lot more than medical doctors or paramedical strength for mental and marital disorders. This feature of our culture has been ignored in the development idea that was thrust on India decades ago.

What We Measure Affects What We Do

Until two decades ago it was not even recognised that high GDP growth does not necessarily mean more jobs. This has been indicated by several studies including those sponsored by the Government. GDP growth does not have as much of an impact on the common person today as it perhaps did four decades ago. Although GDP growth is an important economic measure, it is increasingly becoming irrelevant and even misleading as a political measure, since it impacts only a select few and not the vast majority. Nobel laureate Simon Kuznets, who conceived of GDP initially as a measure of economic performance, never intended it to be the sole economic pursuit and development criteria for a nation, as it has become. He even warned that it should not be a measure of societal well-being. Its value is primarily because it can be used to compare countries rather easily. A compulsive race for GDP growth at all cost can be counter-productive, since it is not a holistic measure of development. As the saying goes, when a measure becomes a target, it ceases to be a good measure. And yet this conception has remained dominant, underpinning research methodology.

There is a saying in statistics, 'everything that counts cannot be counted and everything that can be counted does not count' which succinctly summarises the GDP growth paradox. Short-cut methods with freebies and promises in the name of social welfare and justice are unproductive and politically-driven, but continue to be taken as indicators of development. Has India ever examined such distortions, even as an academic consideration?

Does Development Ensure Social Justice?

Are big dams and huge infrastructure like bullet trains and wide roads in the foothills of the Himalayas, for example, good indictors of development? If so, then at what cost?

To prioritise large-scale infrastructure as an indicator of development falls into the same trap as the earlier example of concrete-roofed houses in villages. The panic created by floods in Joshimath in January 2023, which led to huge cracks in buildings, and roads being washed away, should be a reminder that these markers of 'development' are vulnerable.

An alternative ideal of development should ask, what would sustain 'social security'? The role of family and community cannot be ignored. Similarly, economic growth (as in GDP) and jobs and inequality—all these are constantly changing phenomena, even over the course of an annual study. What is considered 'development' of a nation's people cannot be changing or fluctuating quarterly or year to year. The long-term outlook is forgotten in favour of immediate or short-term criteria because of measurement methodologies, often prompted by political compulsions.

Perhaps India should retrospectively reconsider such measurements and yardsticks to gain a clear picture of the state of the country. This would be the basis of a more durable or sustainable development. Perhaps it is a legacy of colonial rule that empowerment has come to be viewed as externally bestowed instead of being an internal pursuit of individuals. The 'development model' approach, based on exploiting Nature, has come to stay. Should this be the model forever? Many historical Indian kingdoms, such as the Mauryas, Cholas or Vijayanagar empire, had durable governance models. It might be worth considering some of the features of these models as benchmarks for measuring development. Anthropological and even historical research methodologies can include the idea of people's representation, the extent to which it is nurtured or pursued, to bring out the depths of societal change instead of limiting themselves to measuring markets, consumption, opinions, and whatever is obvious.

Archaeological discoveries at Mohenjo Daro and Harappa and later at Hampi, reveal the central role played by community in the past. Civilisations from the Indus Valley onward were based on a cooperative culture and respect for Nature. This communal living ideal has been ignored and replaced with the individual as the unit of thinking and living. That is how numbers have become the basis for measurement today. A quantitative outlook, with comparison and inevitably, competition, has become the dominant paradigm, with the individual eclipsing the community.

As we have seen, successive governments of independent India fell into the trap of emulating the West. In that process, progress is measured by external, exploitative indicators. In this paradigm consumerism is the ultimate measure of development.

To bolster this model of development, the 'research paradigm' measures money-value, mostly quantitatively and on a short time scale, and family values or sharing criteria are not part of the yardstick for development.

Since we adopted the GDP framework and measurement criteria, we have not been able to look beyond it. But we have not even tried to do so. Many Global Indexes rate India very low, but this has not prompted us to re-examine the terms and indices of measurement. The claims of the government make no difference to our ranking year after year. We continue to measure allocations and budgetary proposals and take instant responses to predetermined questions (as in sample surveys) as conclusive. This method of research cannot illuminate the difference policies and interventions have made, or what the citizen and civil society is engaged in, nor the ease of living and human relationships.

Almost a decade ago, Bhutan showed the way with its 'Happiness Index'. In 1922, in his response to winning the Nobel Prize, Albert Einstein proposed that 'a calm and modest life brings more happiness than the constant pursuit of success combined with constant restlessness.' In light of this view, the research framework requires an urgent review as to methodologies and time-frames. We have our own measurement yardsticks; we should be able to exceed any 'global index'. This could be achieved better by a syndicate of independent researchers. But crucial yardsticks like population census, birth and death data and the like are being deferred or disrupted, so that measurement of development indicators becomes blurred—the baseline can be whatever suits the government of the day.

The increasing phenomena of Global Indexes has changed the concerns of national leaders in power or shifted their focus from local developmental concerns to data management aspects, and towards image-management rather than implementation aspects. All this in turn has dampened the country's research potential and credibility.

Is India a 'developed' or 'developing' country? For decades we have claimed to be 'developing' and envisioned a future developed status. At the same time, political leaders claim that India should be a benchmark for other countries in certain respects. This offers an opportunity to evolve an

Indian Index to measure development. The Western research methodologies that we have adopted are predominantly tool-driven, market-oriented, top-down and preoccupied with statistics and surveys, and control and command models. A new research paradigm could look at what a 'New India' requires without succumbing to external models and global compulsions.

In May 2000, Prime Minister Atal Bihari Vajpayee reminded us of our ambiguity about development. Addressing the State Ministers of Environment, he reiterated the 'linkage between human development' and need for 'protecting the environment from mindless consumption and destruction' and cautioned against the 'narrow perceptions' and 'flawed development strategies' of the development model being pursued. And yet governments since then have intensified that pursuit, without pause or reflection.

Fallacy of the Research Paradigm

Development is not merely the budgetary allocation, or number of 'beneficiaries', or the number of bank accounts or proliferation of 'welfare schemes', each with a newer title, as the state broadcaster and official media keep claiming and repeating. Nor is it the length of roads or the number of bridges or flyovers sanctioned, etc. The tendency has been to talk about such schemes individually, not so much their outcome or actual impact over time. Can we recall any outcome finding which has been independently validated on the ground?

Let us examine two flagship programmes about which much has been written and said, as examples. 'Swachh Bharat' is perhaps better described as a campaign. This programme is most recalled in terms of the number of toilets built. But over time, let us say 3 to 5 years after the toilets were built, there has been little lasting effect. Supportive research was carried out and used for publicity including a book by the secretary himself in the garb of an academic exercise.

The government claimed that 'all Indian villages are Open Defecation-Free (ODF)' as a result of its efforts. But soon after that claim was made, four government surveys differed with the government's claim. But the government held on to its claims although four studies by government agencies like the National Statistical Office (NSO), National Annual Rural Sanitation Survey (NARSS), and the National Family Health Survey (NFHS) had revealed that it was only 60-70 per cent of the population who had access to toilets, against the Swachh Survekshan Grameen Survey (in 2021-22) which claimed the population with access to toilets was between 90 and 95 per cent.

Similarly, the MGNREGS (Mahatma Gandhi National Rural Employment Guarantee Scheme) has apparently helped many families, to such an extent that people are waiting for the work provided through the scheme year round. However, many independent spot studies on MGNREGS indicate the rainbow effect. There are no time-series or long-term research to bring out the impact and behaviour change aspects beyond five years. Although, MGNREGS was meant to guarantee work for 100 days initially, on average, it was available for much less. In fact, hardly one-third of those enrolled ever got 100 days of work. The number of days that work was provided for was much less. DWCRA (Development of Women and Children in Rural Areas) is an impressive women's empowerment programme. And it did assist many women. But field research by the School of Rural Studies in Anand indicated that DWCRA schemes are viewed as 'politically manoeuvred'.

Most of the research done on the government's schemes has not been on the overall net results. Studies of the schemes tend to be assessments by the agency which was responsible for implementing the particular scheme or by a government agency which is more concerned with broadcasting the 'achievements' of the government. Now, newer technologies to monitor and remote control will make the illusion of development 'success' even more seductive and deceptive.

After staying in my village continuously for a couple of months, thrice during 2021-23, I wrote a book in Telugu titled 'Should we not be proud of our villages—the example of my village'. When I looked at everything in the village holistically and not as a report to be submitted to a client-Ministry or as an on-the-spot study report, I ended up writing a book. To my satisfaction the book created interest and within three weeks I was invited for talks and discussions of the book in five degree colleges in the district, and was able to educate them on the realities of local development endeavours.

I describe in the book what kind of overall change or impact is obvious and visible. It illustrates how women and 'weaker sections' are reduced to dependents, how the empowerment of women is largely rhetorical, although one scheme did make a visible difference at least for some. There has been a rise in the numbers of women Sarpanches as a result of reservation, although they often remain passive, with their husbands continuing to dominate the decision-making process. The village has been divided more than ever by religion and caste. Political parties have divided people further and kept them that way so that they can retain their hold on vote banks. 'Little Republics', as villages were once known, have become 'colonies' depending on the government for most things. Centralisation has replaced the much-cherished decentralisation, and there has been a proliferation of government agencies. Villages have also become gripped by debt.

I refer to this book of 2022 to illustrate that the kind of development that one sees in the news media and reiterated by political leaders can be illusory. The flaw in the research model can be deceptive, ushering us along the course we are pursuing in the name of development—as if it were an advertising campaign for a consumer product.

The G-20 meet in December 2022 deliberated on 'use of data for public good' in the session on 'Data for Development'. Amitabh Kant, former Chief of NITI Aayog, coordinating this session, announced that 'with the help of data, India had achieved in just three years, the kind of progress that would not have been possible in six decades'. However, the government's frequent reply to many questions in the Parliament to do with social development has been 'no data is available' as if the data can be 'massaged' as and when the government would like it to be. These statements remind us of the kind of dilemma the development paradigm faces today.

In an interview with *Business Standard* in the last week of December 2022, Amitabh Kant observed that, 'so far, in the last 75 years, India has been responding to the developed world. Now we are resetting the agenda. Now we are deciding the priorities of the world.' But Kanti Bajpai, with equally impressive credentials, described Kant's observations as 'hilarious' and wondered 'God only knows what history he (Kant) knows.'

It is obvious that what Amitabh Kant said in the *Business Standard* interview and his lead article in the *Hindustan Times* around the same time, were in support of the PM as the newly-elected G-20 Chair. In this situation, the exaggeration and even disregard of ground realities was at odds with the proposition to other countries that the NITI Aayog 'data management' model is worthy of emulation. The Data Protection Bill, in violation of the right to privacy and RTI (Right to Information) provisions, is set to gain Parliament's approval. Kant was trying to justify this Act using the G-20 as backdrop. But, considering the senior and responsible positions involved, this episode serves to illustrate the government's perspective on development.

3

GLOBAL INDEXES AND RESEARCH CREDIBILITY

Where Is An Indian Model?

As we have seen, a 'foreign research model' has taken root and become the benchmark, and with it, rating and ranking has become the new yardstick not only for research methodologies but even for 'development'. This is based on administrative data from within which is, often, collected by the same people responsible for implementation. The basis for rating is relative—in most cases, the rating model does not recognise the local peculiarities, initiatives and innovative practices. Rather it is the numbers and macro interests which matter and dictate the priorities for the research methodology and report aggregation. Such methodologies promote a 'macho outlook' with quantifiable indicators prioritised over experiences, experiments and expectations. This kind of rating and ranking suits populism, centralisation and the 'control and command' policies of the global powers. It is in their interests that certain algorithms are used to justify and perpetuate certain tools. Global indexes are one such tool. This approach reflects the macro interests, global hegemony and market expansion strategies of those in power. Many of the indices and methodologies are being used to homogenise countries as part of one, global, market.

It is worth recalling three approaches from earlier decades to appraise the recent changes in the social and economic system. The social science model was based on 'participatory reports', oriented towards an understanding and appreciation of local practices. Mahatma Gandhi was an applied social researcher. His ideas and concerns were first sounded with the stakeholders who were on the receiving end, experimented with first at the micro level, and then assessed for future implications. Dr Martin Luther King, Jr, too, used this approach. Only after these steps was the initial idea modified and put through formal committees for further deliberation and adoption regionally, without ignoring local civil society. This was before social science methodology had taken root formally. The more recent initiatives of Nanaji Deshmukh and Bunker Roy, for example, could be described as an Indian model of development.

This Indian model can be described as participatory or action-oriented and objective (with no conflict of interest), with no intention of submerging local identities. The use of case studies brings out these characteristics vividly. Some rankings and rating models are briefly discussed, to bring out their limits. Ratings are used to show what difference has been made to stakeholders and what interventions have been facilitated.

Transparency International (TI) is one of the global

agencies promoting and popularising rating and ranking research. In this case, their index is on levels of corruption in countries. Their ranking methodology is informally endorsed by organisations like the World Bank (TI is run by ex-World Bank professionals), and is taken note of by countries. The Indian government's concern is increasingly on how to better the ranking given in the TI Index rather than addressing the phenomenon of corruption itself in all its complexity at the micro level. For this, the measures taken are macro level claims. In contrast to this approach, the Indian PEE (Perceptions, Experience and Estimate) model developed by CMS in 2002, which has a higher reliability than the TI, provides insights for intervention at multiple levels to effectively address corruption. While the TI Index is based solely on a small, unrepresentative sample, PEE involves multiple methodologies (sample surveys, past data analysis, observations, case studies, and discussions with key stakeholders.) This methodology offers not only a better understanding of the phenomenon with a wider perspective but provides suggestions for sustaining initiatives to minimise the scope of corruption—unlike in the case of a ranking model. Corruption in India cannot be approached with an instant formula or surface-scratching initiatives. Corruption involves social-psychological-cultural behaviour. This cannot be addressed through the rating or ranking approach.

The Citizen Report Card and Social Audit are two examples of locally developed alternate research methodologies. Dr Samuel Paul, a former Director of IIM, Ahmedabad, on his retirement to Bangalore, initiated the Citizen Report Card in 1994 at his Public Affairs Centre.

This report card methodology has been well demonstrated to foster accountability in the delivery of public services. The Social Audit and PEE methodologies developed and demonstrated by myself between 1993-2010, engage and involve citizens, educate them in availing basic public services and even in correcting the functioning of these services. Going beyond monitoring or feedback, these methodologies give deep insights into local initiatives. These methodologies also promote collective sensitivities. Despite the existence of such initiatives within the country, little recognition or validation has been given to them.

Indexing is a macro-level tool to measure and track change, performance and implementation or accomplishment. Indexes and ranking, when accompanied by stakeholders' perspectives, can be useful. Indexes are based on a range of indicators which are related or somewhat linked. The strength of these linkages is determined based on data reliability and prior research. A good example is the 'India child-well-being index' of August 2019, by a non-profit agency. Based on 24 indicators, it provided insights on health, nutrition, education, sanitation and child protection indicators. Releasing this report, NITI Aayog CEO Amitabh Kant noted that the index offers an opportunity to states to come up with new initiatives and interventions wherever correctives or adjustments in policies or implementation are required. Indicators in the index could be interrogated for their relevance or inter-relationship. This would help the index improve in the next round. This provision for openness, and explanation of the assumptions and basis of research, is laudable.

The National Crime Research Bureau has brought out

an annual report for some years with data on a range of deviant behaviours in the country. This report offers a wealth of data for social researchers to explore trends, causes and consequences on a wide range of issues and interrelationships. With the support of social researchers, this report could be made into a vital source for the Government to take initiatives against various kinds of crime. For this, the report must give desegregated data and make an effort to go beyond typical 'administrators' data'. It must also avoid being influenced by the political interests of the day, like changes in definitions without explanation, and adjusting the period of the data covered. The NCRB report itself is unlikely to be annual as the decadal national census missed its regularity in 2021.

The ASER (Annual Status of Education Report) and NFHS (National Family Health Survey) reports, involving case studies, trend analyses, field sample surveys and ranking of states, is yet another research model being used. These reports serve to flag the trends in general and specific contexts. And since they are conducted independently with a public service concern, they have become better potential tools as of 2023. They offer proactive initiatives at micro and macro levels instead of remaining a bureaucratic exercise.

Going by these independent research initiatives, the country should have questioned the Global Indexes at the very outset, and resisted prescriptions based on the formulas or algorithms which serve the interests of a few countries, however powerful they may be. We should have pointed out that no one model or definition fits all countries, and that it is hegemonic to impose such models. In fact, that should have been the stand of India decades earlier in the case of the prescriptive conditions of the World Bank, IMF or UNDP. Even better, India should have proposed an alternative approach to the global indexes, service or sector wise, for other countries to help themselves without losing their own identity, cultural roots and local compulsions.

India has two unique strands of history that should not be ignored as global indexes tend to do. The first is our long civilizational history, as it informs our 'identities and insights'. The second is the independent stand India took in the immediate post-colonial years, lasting over thirty years (1940-1970) when we had even questioned UNESCO's prescription (1970-75) of what qualified as 'developed'. From this position of strength, India is now in a more vulnerable position, in part due to the selective acknowledgement of global indexes by Indian leaders. When India's rank in the global index on innovation 'improved' by a few positions, for example, in July 2019, our Prime Minister referred to it to claim advancement for India. In November 2022, when India's rank showed a further increase, the Prime Minister pointed this out again as if it was a certificate for India, and as a result of which we have legitimised the Global Index. The President of India referred to this the same index again in her address to the Parliament in January 2023. At the Davos economic conference in January 2023, the CEO of NITI Aayog, Parameswaran Iyer, a brilliant bureaucrat, too referred to India's position on the Global Index to showcase India's achievement by citing the score on 'ease of doing business' (from 142 a few years ago to 62 in 2022). After that, can India denigrate Global Indexes?

Proliferating Number of Global Indexes

There has been a mushrooming of Global Indexes in recent years, and there are now more than two dozen in active circulation globally. At one time there were nearly a hundred such ratings and rankings. Some of them, like the ones on democracy, freedom, hunger and environment, are talked about more than others. Some, like the ones on 'freedom' are three decades old, and most others have existed for two decades. Most of them originate in the USA, a few are from the UK or the Netherlands, Sweden and Germany. Why none originate in India is curious. Perhaps none of the research pioneers in India felt it worthwhile to devote their effort to this global pursuit as they were not sure of funding or the difference these macro-level indexes make, given the wide differences in socio-cultures and political systems of countries. Together these different indexes reflect broadly the development, democracy and governance issues across the globe.

An index is a research exercise, each with its own combination of data, analytics, surveys, select discussions, tracking and monitoring of inputs. A Global Index gives a rank to countries on the basis of the score they reach in the index's algorithm or methodology. The ranking of countries is presented, giving the rank of number one to the country which scored highest on the preselected variables and a higher number to the country which scored low or least on the selected variables and criteria for that year. For example, on the Environment Performance Index, the World Bank and Yale University in 2023 ranked India the last, that is 180 out of 180 countries covered. On the Climate Change Performance

Index, the German Watch NGO ranked India at 8 out of 59 countries it covered for 2023. Why is there so much difference between these two indexes on India's environment ranking? To understand, we need to match the variables, the definitions and base lines used and methodologies depended on.

An algorithm or formula is promoted as a means to find a desirable norm when in fact it is a set of equations based on data manipulation. The methodology is justified as being neutral when it is in fact to the advantage of certain powers who are in a position to promote their model. Even international forums, like the UN and World Bank, push their own algorithms. Although a few experts knew of the politics behind the algorithms, the credit for articulating the issues goes to an Indian expert, Rajiv Malhotra.

While some global indexes like, for example, that on Press Freedom, continue to be devised by stakeholder activists, most others were promoted by one or other global funding or lending agency, directly or indirectly, perhaps by their former executives. This includes the World Bank, IMF, and even the UN bodies. In fact, two or three much talked about global indexes are by a UN agency like UNDP, and at least two are by the World Bank itself. Some agencies are think-tanks of academic origin, a couple are activist agencies crusading for issues like human rights, or freedom of press or gender. They all try to influence socio-political and economic policies of countries. The *Economist* publication, which has credibility and an extensive database, comes up with a global index on more than two subjects. Some global index or the other gets released at the Davos economic conference annually. Some of these indexes enjoy wide media coverage globally and even get debated in domestic decision-making bodies. Some cannot hide their ideological leanings. Global PR agencies are the latest to join this global game by supporting one or other prestigious academic (like the Wharton School) or news group (like US News). Identifying the 'best country in the world' is an example of how these global indexes of late have become a lobbying exercise.

What difference these indexes have made to countries is not known. I have not come across any independent research study on what impact these indexes have made at any level. Of course it is talked about that they influence international perceptions and even national affairs and help some power in its push and pull manoeuvres over some advantage, political or economic. For example, some powers expect adjustments in national policies both economic and political, and they expect to set global benchmarks as per their own concerns and interests. The influence of any global index has not been documented, which is interesting, given how they are used to leverage economic interests or push forward consumerism or other interests of big global powers and corporate conglomerates. Some indexes appear to be bound up in these powers' 'arm-twisting' tactics or even bullying strategies.

These Global Indexes pose a challenge to researchers in India, more than to the Indian Government. They offer an opportunity to researchers and remind them of the pioneering role of Indian mathematicians, statisticians, analysts, managers and economists have made in policy formulation and appraisal. But researchers too seem to regard global indexes in the same way as successive governments, as criticism, instead of as an opportunity for global leadership and further research. As someone who was involved in India's early ranking exercise on banking (customer) services in 1994 and more than a decade later in ranking management institutes (along with Kamla Choudhary and N.C.B. Nath), these global indexes intrigued me. Why had no one in India started some such exercise, of rating the countries on their policies or growth trends? Perhaps because researchers were initially engrossed in 'developmental research'. They then slowly slipped into serving political interests or supporting corporate campaigns. Perhaps Indian research had an undercurrent of cooperative spirit, rather than the competitive outlook which propelled the early global indexes. But India missed an opportunity. Proliferating global indexes now pose a challenge to both the government and researchers. Today few countries, outside the US, have the research potential to credibly question the methodologies used by these various global indexes. India could have mobilised an alternative framework to promote a consultation-driven ranking of countries. Indian research infrastructure has this potential. This would have been a good basis to claim that the next decade and beyond belongs to India.

But at the same time we need to be able to handle a multiplicity of data sources, variable quality or reliability of data and of course, a wide range of estimates. For example, we have five different estimates of the number of people below the poverty line, using different sources and threshold levels. As a result, these estimates range as widely as some Global Indexes. If governments consider that a lack of updated data is better in order to claim whatever suits them, it is no wonder that the credibility of government claims is often dubious.

How India Is Ranked in Different Global Indexes: An Overview from 2022

S.No	Global Index	India's Rank/ countries covered
1	Environmental Performance	180/180
2	Press Freedom	161/180
3	Happiness	126/137
4	Gender Gap	135/146
5	Human Development	132/191
6	Inequalities	123/161
7	Human Freedom	112/165
8	Liveability	112/173
9	Hunger	107/121
10	Corruption	85/180
11	Rule of Law	77/140
12	Food Security	68/113

Global indexes presuppose that countries should have a similar approach towards development, democracy and governance. Global funding agencies as well as the powers behind them expect other nations to follow a prescribed model of development or growth. But as was evident in the 2022 Davos conference deliberations, the key players now realise that it is not practical to expect countries to fall in line behind one model of development. This realisation should be welcomed and should be reflected in the methodologies being followed.

In two different indexes to do with democracy, conducted by three different research agencies, one from the UK and the other from Sweden, India has been placed at 93/179 and 46/167, respectively. Even a third agency, Freedom House of the US, described India as 'flawed' or 'failed' among the countries covered. The three agencies have not explained the circumstances for such wide differences in their ranking. All three classify Indian democracy adversely with different labels like 'flawed' and 'partly free', which reflects their ideological differences.

The Environmental Performance Index by Yale and Columbia Universities, funded by the World Bank and based on 40 parameters, showed India at 180th place out of 180 countries covered. The Environmental Performance Index report for 2022 explained how India had slipped further to the 'sluggish' level, because on many of the parameters, in 11 issue categories, the decline in performance had continued. The argument of the Indian Government was that 'environment and ecological security are a luxury and cannot be prioritised ahead of human development'. It has long claimed that human development is separate from the environment.

India has rejected the methodology of the Environmental Performance Index, claiming that for a developing country, an 'accurate method' of ranking should be based on per capita greenhouse gas emissions. It is obvious that the two US Universities do not consider the Indian data on renewable energy as reliable. Also, they track the related policy measures and changes in the implementation much more closely, whereas the government relies for data on the same agencies responsible for implementation of the policy. When news reports and environmental activists point out that government decisions lead to lack of environmental protection, and are the basis for India's low rank, this is met with hostility by the government. The news media coverage in January 2023 of cracks in houses and public roads in Uttarakhand following floods, was viewed as one example of this conflict. We seem to be falling into the trap of floating fake indexes to counter global indexes, but this will not lead to solutions.

In October 2022, the government rejected the Global Hunger Index (India ranked 107 out of 121 countries covered), alleging that it was 'a deliberate attempt to taint India's image' and that the report 'lowers India's rank' on the basis of a 'minuscule' sample of 3000 respondents. The Ministry stated that the index ignored an 'increase in per capita dietary energy supply' and the food security efforts of the government, including during the pandemic period. Commenting on the index, Professor Dipa Sinha of Ambedkar University said that the schemes and initiatives of the government had 'helped ease the hunger situation, but fell short of being adequate'. It is clear that three of the four indicators used by the index are related to the health of young children, not the total population. On December 9, 2022, in reply to a question in Parliament, the Minister claimed that there was 'no report of starvation deaths from the states'. The Minister should have used the opportunity to clarify the complexity of the situation, rather than avoiding the issue.

Apart from describing the Index on democracy as 'misleading, incorrect and misplaced', the Government gave no explanation of the research methodology or the indices used by the three agencies or their sources. In fact, when a member of the Rajya Sabha asked a question, the Minister wrote to the Chairman of the House requesting that the question be disallowed as it was 'sensitive', 'trivial' and that it was done 'without consulting any government agencies'. The Economist Intelligence Unit, one of the three agencies involved, revealed that the Indian Government attempted to engage them on the ranking 'without being forthcoming with any data or logic'. What do such responses of the Government indicate? They indicate that we have no experts, academic institutes and independent research on these various indices to respond coherently, credibly and adequately.

In most of these Global Indexes, the trend has been more or less consistent, as if things in India have either remained the same or have deteriorated in recent years. Or, perhaps it is the methodology and the data sources that have remained constrained. The Government has been claiming an altogether contrary situation, or the official data available gives a different picture. How can this be? Neither the Indian Government nor any research body has come up with any clarification or explanation for this ambiguous situation. What is at stake is the credibility of Government data and we seem to have not taken any initiative in this regard.

Theme Categories of Global Indexes

The thirty-three global indexes reviewed for this book are grouped into six categories. The United Nations, World Bank and their affiliates are involved with at least one index in each group and at least one US-based agency is responsible for at least two indexes in each group. Activists/professionals are involved in at least two indexes in each of these six groups.

Grouping of Prominent Global Indexes with Number of Countries Covered and the Rank of India in Each Case with the Agency in Brackets (2022-23)

Freedom/Democracy	
Relevant Index	**Rank**
Freedom in the World (Freedom House)	66/100
Democracy (EIU)	46/167
Democracy (V-DEM)	108/179
Human Freedom (Cato Institute and the Fraser Institute)	112/165
Economic Freedom (The Heritage Foundation)	131/177
Corruption (Transparency International Britain based NGO)	85/180
Press Freedom (Reporters without Borders)	161/180

Governance	
Relevant Index	**Rank**
Ease of doing business (World Bank)	63/190
Governance (World Bank) *(*WB has since discontinued)*	111/214
Rule of law (World Justice Project (WJP))	79/142
Peace (Institute for Economics & Peace (IEP))	126/163
Terrorism (Institute for Economics & Peace (IEP))	13/163
Competitiveness (Institute for Management Development (IMD), Switzerland)	40/64

Development/Life Standards	
Relevant Index	**Rank**
Human Development (UNDP)	132/191
Happiness (Sustainable Development Solutions Network)	126/137
Liveability (EIU)	141/173
Hunger (Concern Worldwide, Ireland, and Welthungerhilfe, Germany)	111/125
Food Security (The British weekly The Economist)	68/113

Environment	
Relevant Index	**Rank**
Environment performance (World Bank Yale University)	180/180
Climate Change Performance (Three Environmental NGOs German Watch, New Climate Institute and Climate Action Network)	**8/59**
Best country in the World (US News & World Report, BAV Group, and the Wharton School of the University of Pennsylvania)	30/87

Social Development	
Relevant Index	**Rank**
Gender Gap (The World Economic Forum (WEF))	127/146
Reducing in Inequality (Oxfam International and Development Finance International (DFI))	123/161
Social Progress (Economic Advisory Council to the Prime Minister (EAC-PM))	110/169
Kids Rights (Kids Rights Foundation)	115/193
Minority (Patna-based research institute Centre for Policy Analysis (CPA))	**1/110**

Tech based	
Relevant Index	**Rank**
Innovation (World Intellectual Property Organization)	40/132
Talent Competitiveness (INSEAD, collaboration with human resource firm Adecco and Google)	101/133
Logistics Index (World Bank)	38/139
Intellectual Property (US Chambers of Commerce)	42/55
Digital Quality of Life (A cybersecurity firm, Surfshark, Netherlands)	52/121
Passport (Financial advisory services firm Arton Capital, Canada)	144/199

The score given to India in the indexes differs widely from one index to the other within each category and in all the six groups. Of course, the indexes in each group are not based on exactly the same indicators or methodology. But they belong to the same theme category and thus examine similar issues.

Number of Countries Covered and India's Rank

Six Categories	Number of countries covered, range between	India's rank, range between different index
Freedom/Democracy	85 – 180	150 – 46
Development/ Life standards	113 – 191	136 – 68
Social Development	110 – 169	135 – 1
Governance	63 – 214	135 – 12
Environment/ Climate	59 – 180	180 – 59
Technology related	63 – 193	101 – 40

Why does the number of countries covered by various indexes within the same theme category vary so much? Is it to do with the resources available to the agency concerned or is it to do with availability of data and convenience of ranking certain countries (by dropping or adding countries)? For example, German Watch covered 59 countries and showed India as 8th in rank, whereas the World Bank-supported Environmental Performance Index covered 180 countries and put India at 180th position. Why has environment/climate change attracted four different indexes, democracy three and innovation and competitiveness themes attracted two global indexes each?

The rank given to India varies considerably within particular theme categories of global indexes. For example, in the Governance category group, India was ranked at 135 on 'peace' and at 13 on 'terrorism'. Both covered 163-164 countries. This brings out the extent of subjective consideration. Data from the same source or with the same basis cannot yield so much variation.

An analysis of India's rank over recent years further indicates that perhaps the rank reflects that little was accomplished in the country during those years. Or has there been a steadily declining course?

But on the other hand, some of these global indexes released annually show a difference in the score year-to-year as if during that year some change took place in the country and that change was revealed by their analysis or research. For example, on the 'Corruption Index', the year-to-year change for India was around three points, while the total number of countries covered remained the same. In the case of the 'Human Freedom Index', the score for India varied from 7 to 16 points. This variation is probably due to subjective interpretation of the country-specific sources relied upon. As can be seen from the table, India's score went up (the situation worsened) from 94 in 2020 to 119 out of 165 countries covered in 2021. On the Democracy Index, India's score went up from 32 in 2016, out of 165 countries covered, to 53 in 2020. The explanation given for this change is not based on specific quantitative or policy interventions. But in some cases, it was apparently local news reports which influenced the score in the index and perceptions about the reliability of data.

In the Hunger Index, India has been on a steadily declining course for the last 7 to 8 years. Going by this index, Sri Lanka, Nepal, China, Brazil and Russia have been doing better than India consistently in the last seven years.

How India has been ranked over the years: Five examples.

Year	**Corruption Perception Index** (by Transparency International)	**Human Freedom Index** (by Cato Institute)	**Democracy Index** (by EIU)	**Liberal Democracy Index (LDI)** (by V-DEM)	**Economic Freedom Index (EFI)** (by Heritage Foundation)
2015	76/168	75/152	35/167	–	128/178
2016	79/176	87/159	32/167	–	123/178
2017	81/180	102/159	42/167	70/174	143/180
2018	78/180	110/162	41/167	81/178	130/180
2019	80/180	94/162	51/167	85/179	129/180
2020	86/180	111/162	53/167	90/179	120/180
2021	85/180	119/165	46/167	97/179	121/184
2022	85/180	112/165	46/167	93/179	131/177

How countries have been ranked in the global index on hunger over the years

Number of Countries	2023	2022	2019	2018	2017	2016	2015
Countries covered	**125**	**121**	**117**	**119**	**119**	**118**	**117**
India	***111***	***107***	***102***	***103***	***100***	***97***	***93***
China	1-20	1-17	25	25	29	29	26
Brazil	32	20	18	31	18	1-16	22
Sri Lanka	60	64	66	67	84	84	82
Nepal	69	81	73	72	72	72	71
Pakistan	102	99	94	106	106	107	106
Russia	26	28	22	21	22	24	24

Source: GHI

Bias against India is too obvious from this table. Perhaps the agency is taking the data provided by those countries on face value, but not the Indian data.

Most global indexes are based on multiple sources of data, field surveys and in some cases, expert assessments and news media sources. The data is gathered from time to time and in some cases includes data put out by the concerned government agency or their networks. The time reference is not always compatible in every respect but the year is indicated in the index. All the indexes give the basis and the methodology used. Most of them indicate the criteria and indices used for arriving at the weightages of individual countries. Not much is indicated about the kind of sample surveys conducted or the experts who were consulted. A few indexes even discuss or explain the changes in their methodology from time to time. It is obvious from these explanations that newspaper reports, sample surveys and expert opinions carried more weight where credible independent data sources are not available for the country. That seems to increasingly be the case with India.

Not much is known about the reaction of other countries to these global indexes and their ranking over the years. Is the Indian Government the only one protesting, contesting or ignoring the index? Why has India never taken up this issue at any of the bilateral or regional meetings? How else can the agencies responsible for the indexes be held accountable, and their flaws exposed?

On the face of it, it is intriguing that most indexes, irrespective of the agency and methodology used, depict India in a poor light (as can be seen in the tables). The credibility of government sources or their data appears to be a factor.

Of course, considering the unique character of a country, as in the case of India, it is difficult for a global index to reflect the ground realities and changes year to year.

Over all, not every index could be said to be equally objective to all the countries covered. In fact, for some countries the concepts used and the data or statistics used may not be appropriate and may even be distortive. However authentic the data sources may be, they could never be neutral as is claimed by most countries. Unless transparency is evident throughout and there was a prior consultation process, it must be considered that some of the base assumptions behind the indexes are rooted in colonialism.

In fact, some two decades ago or more, the whole idea of the global index was prompted by international funding agencies to help them formulate lending policies and even help leverage loan conditions with obligations. That was how global indexes evolved, instituted by retired professionals of those international economic bodies like the World Bank, IMF, etc., with the assistance of one or the other academic institutes for research backup and to justify the claim of 'independent' or 'think-tank' research. The indexes on corruption, democracy, development, freedom, hunger, environment, etc., originated that way, with subjectivity. The subjective element cannot of course be avoided altogether, but transparency in the exercise and acknowledging limitations enhances the index's relevance.

Those agencies who had credible research back up, data bases, academic facilities and faculties took to the global index exercise seriously. A few of them were also engaged in fundamental research, as in the case of reputed universities. The claim of being 'independent' too helped in that pursuit.

While one cannot expect indexes to be relevant equally to all countries being covered, there is a definite trend of showing India way below average score or rank, in over two dozen global indexes, although they were conducted by different agencies. This deserves a serious review by credible independent experts in India. In the last couple of years, only one global index (on Climate Change Performance) has showed India within the top 10 rank.

Since these global indexes play a role in shaping perceptions and can even influence international affairs, they need to be analysed squarely, particularly when they continue to present a bleak picture year after year. Even more so, when it is not one index as in the case of democracy, freedom or environment, but three global indexes which continue to rank India low, with labels like 'electoral autocratic', 'flawed', 'decaying', 'black sliding', 'all-time low', 'illiberal democracy', etc. On democracy in India, for example, these ranks get used by academics globally and become a reference point.

The Freedom House Index on freedom/democracy is funded by the US Government and has been operational since 1973 in one form or another. Today they base their ranking on 25 different dimensions including the narrative dimension. This has the scope for bringing in its own ideological orientation in the ranking of India. The dimensions include journalistic freedom, religious representation, academic freedom, etc., which can rely on anecdotal evidence and reports in different news media.

The *Economist* magazine brings its editorial stance to bear in compiling the ranking of democracies. Its 2021 report discussed democracy in India as 'decaying', 'back sliding', and having 'reached an all-time low'. Its emphases on the citizenship amendment Act during that year, as well as the PM laying the foundation of a religious temple might have swayed the weightage. It is evident that the consideration is subjective, political or ideological.

The V-DEM index of the Democracy Institute at the University of Gothenburg relies on statistics of organisations like USAID, the World Bank and other academic studies including Human Rights Watch. It too takes a certain editorial stand on countries and stated in its 2020 report that 'India has continued on a path of steep decline to the extent that it has almost lost its status as a democracy.' It reclassified India as an 'electoral autocracy', and noted a decline in 'the autonomy of the election management' based on a news report of 66 retired civil servants decrying the Election Commission of India. It also took account of the 'diminishing sensitivity of freedom of expression', going by certain media reports. The March 2023 observations of the Supreme Court on independence of the Election Commission of India are likely to be taken as the basis for 2023 and 2024 rounds of the index.

V-DEM Example

The V-DEM index on Liberal Democracy covers 179 countries and is based on five indicators ('Liberal', 'Electoral', 'Egalitarian', 'Participatory' and 'Deliberative'). On all these five variables, India's rank is similar, but it varies between the five. Under 'egalitarian' it continues to be much lower. India has showed a decline in ranking in the last few years on all the five parameters—from around 75 to 118 in 2017 to around 73 to 123 for 2023.

V-DEM's Ranking of India in Its Democracy Index on Five Components

Year	Liberal Democracy Index (LDI)	Electoral Component	Liberal Component	Egalitarian Component	Participatory Component	Deliberative Component
2017	**70/174**	73/174	76/174	118/174	62/174	76/174
2018	**81/178**	82/178	78/178	110/178	82/178	128/178
2019	**85/179**	87/179	70/179	118/179	84/179	102/179
2020	**90/179**	89/179	93/179	122/179	105/179	145/179
2021	**97/179**	101/179	88/179	124/179	91/179	126/179
2022	**93/179**	100/179	69/179	114/179	85/179	102/179
2023	**97/179**	108/179	90/179	123/179	73/179	95/179

Source: V-DEM annual reports

The sanctity of 'liberal', 'egalitarian' and 'deliberative' for democracy cannot be universal. How can countries with different Constitutions be compared on such ambiguous criteria? Also, this table for 2017 to 2023 brings out the fact that even V-DEM apparently relies more on subjective assessment and on newspaper reports to arrive at a quantitative score on all these indicative components.

It is likely that ideological and political orientations are being overplayed, and the foundational strengths of Indian democracy are being ignored. News media reports seem to be selectively used to deviate from quantification and empirical research of the index. But, crucially, this should have been overcome with independent and transparent research within the country. Independent institutions engaged in such research and analysis should have been at the forefront to repudiate the rankings.

The Press Freedom Index by Reporters Without Borders ranked India in 2023 in the bottom quarter of countries covered. An Advisory Committee of the Cabinet Secretary referred to the Indian ranking as 'arbitrary', 'perception-based', 'non-credible' and 'not tenable'. This Committee requested that the World Bank demand that the agencies conducting Global Indexes show 'greater transparency and accountability'. Instead of limiting this request to the three agencies who have been ranking India low in their democracy index, the position could have been wider. An analysis of the 60-plus indicators on our terms of objectivity should have been validated by an independent research institute.

A New Tool

A review of some of the indexes (like on freedom, and democracy) over a ten-year period indicates that the change that is reflected in the rank of India year to year is based more on 'contentious policies', reflecting what the news media presents from their own perspective, or based on data bases and unrepresentative sample surveys. The change in rank is not always based on the position on the ground at the time. That a change in some public policies is normal in an electoral mandate is not adequately considered in the ranking of India year to year. Also, the decline of independent and credible sources of data and evaluative research in the country in recent years has been useful for the agency compiling the index, giving it more credibility.

Global Indexes attempt to create homogeneity between geographically, culturally and politically independent countries. The number of indexes has been expanding,

> sometimes into civilizational and cultural roots of countries. They seem to have become tools of foreign policy. They nurture notions of 'superiority' and 'inferiority', ignoring distinctions which cannot be measured. They prompt a competitive culture in the name of 'sustainability', widening the gap between sovereign nations and divides within.
>
> Thus, while the relevance of an index is temporal and linked to public policy, they could nevertheless be used by governments as 'early warning systems' or for course correctives from within. A country like India, with strengths which cannot be measured by such tools, should evolve its own strategies by strengthening and unleashing its own independent research institutes, culture and practices. It is the complacency of the country that has let it down. India should gear up and project its own model based on its own strengths.

India's Ambiguous Response

As we have just seen, the various global indexes each have their own flaws and biases. This should not blind us to the fact that India's own research lacks credibility. The best way to deal with India's poor ranking in global indexes is through consultation and serious and credible research. Instead, the government's response has been bureaucratic or political. India today has the best of brains even within the NITI Aayog on data, statistical analysis and research methodologies. Yet we have not examined the definitions, the methodologies used, the structure of data and composite score arrived at in the case of each global index. Clearly the government is not prepared to face the issue, despite the effect of the poor ratings on India's global standing. There are rumours about the government's attempts to tackle the ratings by informally reaching out to the research agency involved. There are also attempts to float dummy agencies outside the country or inside, to put out an alternative index on the same theme as the one with an unfavourable rating.

The NITI Aayog is best placed to take on the task of analysing global indexes and respond where necessary. The DMEO (Development Monitoring and Evaluation Office) in the NITI Aayog was supposed to be the nodal point for all such reviews and initiatives. It has been collecting parameters used in different Global Indexes for a few years, following a review by the Cabinet Secretary in January 2020, 'with a view to improve India's ranking in the Global Index'. Since then, however, in many of those indexes, India's ranking has declined. To deal with this decline, the concerned Ministry was expected to examine the appropriateness of the data used for the particular index. For example, the Law Ministry's Legislative department was supposed to look into India's ranking on the Democracy Index. The NITI Aayog was supposed to have virtual workshops with 47 Union Ministries in this regard. However, no action plan to better India's ranking has emerged. It is obvious that instead of engaging subject experts from outside, the government continues to deal bureaucratically with the issue, which has made no difference so far.

India is known to have high calibre academics and credible independent research outfits with impressive track records. Why are they not being involved? Why is there hardly any example of the agencies engaged in compiling global indexes availing of Indian expertise? There is no news of their involvement in report writing or analysis or validation or even for a review.

The trend of India's ranking in global indexes should also concern Indian scientists, researchers and academia. The annual National Science Congress, which meets in January, and is inaugurated by the Prime Minister, has never deliberated, even in the side-lines, about the significance of global indexes and what they mean for the country's overall achievement and scientific pursuit. Even professional and academic associations like political scientists, sociologists, anthropologists or economists have never looked into the methodology of global indexes even as an academic exercise. Perhaps they were never approached by any of the government agencies within the country. Why has the NITI Aayog not prompted academics to examine any global index?

India Today's Early Initiatives

There are many early examples as pointed in the table of governments missing an opportunity to develop an Indian framework for a global index. I recall three early examples. Two decades ago (2003), *India Today* magazine with Laveesh Bhandari and Bibek Debroy sensitised political leaders in India with their annual rating of states based on their own field studies together with state-specific data in the public domain. This report made political leaders and state governments conscious of the heights they could aspire to in different spheres of development and governance. This index alerted leaders about performance outcomes and even helped leaders come up with initiatives. In 2022, India Today–MDRA (Marketing and Development Research Associates) did rigorous and comprehensive research. *India Today's State of the States of India 2022* with 12 parameters and 189 indicators is an example of an Indian independent Performance Index with empirical evidence. This index has become something of a 'success mantra' for Chief Ministers to take on and follow up.

As a pioneer research and advocacy organisation, CSE (Centre for Science and Environment) has been well acknowledged for its comprehensive annual report 'State of India's Environment'. It offers a credible review of the environment scenario state-wise to enable local initiatives proactively. CSE's Transparency Index (a rating of pollution control boards on their public disclosures) is another example published in CSE's own magazine.

Based on two decades of field research, CMS devised an annual assessment of whether citizens were availing of basic public services with a PEE (Perception, Experience and Estimation) model using a range of methodologies. Based on a large sample survey and discussions with service providers, it rated states on corruption involving citizens and the exercise enabled initiatives and intervention by concerned local authorities.

Some Examples of Ranking/Index Agencies in India

Year	Indexes	Agencies
2021	National e-Governance Service Delivery Assessment (NeSDA), (2nd Edition)	Released by Union Minister. Department of Administrative Reforms and Public Grievances (DARPG)
2022	State Energy and Climate Index (SECI), (Round 1)	NITI Aayog
2022	District Good Governance Index (DGGI), (J & K)	Index has prepared by Department of Administrative Reforms and Public Grievances (DARPG)
2019-20	**Healthy States, Progressive India** (Fourth Edition of State Health Index)	NITI Aayog
2021	Good Governance Index (GGI)	Launched by Union Minister of Home Affairs and Minister of Cooperation. Department of Administrative Reforms and Public Grievances (DARPG)
2021	National Multidimensional Poverty Index (MPI)	NITI Aayog
2021	IPF Smart Policing Index	Indian Police Foundation (IPF)
2023	Air Quality Index (AQI)	Central Pollution Control Board (CPCB)
2022	Public Affairs Index (PAI), (7th Edition)	Public Affairs Centre (PAC)
2021	School Education Quality Index (SEQI)	NITI Aayog
2021-22	FSSAI's 4th State Food Safety Index (SFSI)	Ministry of Health and Family Welfare
2022	National Institutional Ranking Framework (NIRF)	Ministry of Education, GoI
2019	Composite Water Management Index 2.0 (CWMI)	NITI Aayog
2022	Financial Inclusion Index (FI-Index)	Reserve Bank of India (RBI)
2021	Health Index of India	NITI Aayog
2021	'Transparency Index: Rating of Pollution Control Boards on Public Disclosure'	Centre for Science and Environment (CSE)
2020-21	Performance Grading Index (PGI)	Department of School Education and Literacy, Ministry of Education
2020-21	3rd Sustainable Development Goals (SDG) India Index	NITI Aayog
2022	India Innovation Index	NITI Aayog
2022	Ease of Living Index (EoLI)	Minister of Housing and Urban Affairs
2022	Data Governance Quality Index (DGQI)	Development Monitoring and Evaluation Office (DMEO), NITI Aayog
2023	IMD Smart City Index Report (SCI Report)	Smart City Observatory (SCO) / Institute for Management Development (IMD)
2022	State Energy & Climate Index (Round – I)	NITI Aayog (Gujarat)
2022	4th Health Index	NITI Aayog (Kerala)
2002-20	India Corruption Ratings Annual	CMS (Rating Status on citizen availing public services)
2004-12	Best & Worst states of India	India Today – Bibek Debroy & Laveesh Bhandari
2000-2023	State of India's Environment	Centre for Science and Environment (CSE)
2022	State of States of India 2022	By MDRA-India Today
2005-2017	Corruption in availing public services by citizen	CMS
2019-2020	Ranking of coaching/institutes	MDRA – India Today

A NITI Aayog Initiative—Ranking States

The NITI Aayog for some years has been engaged in offering a series of indexes on performance of the states on various themes. Some of them are conducted annually as if to foster a competitive spirit between states. It should be said that the NITI Aayog ranking of the states has galvanised the bureaucracies in the states and made them more outcome-oriented in the last couple of years. However, the NITI Aayog's initiatives in this regard would have been far more effective if the exercise were more transparent and consultation based, and involved independent experts too. Instead of allowing the ranking to be viewed as a bureaucratic exercise, the Aayog should have engaged independent professional bodies, including academic institutes, in compiling the index at state level, at least to review the methodologies. Some states have in turn taken up ranking of their districts on similar lines. Those states which see these ratings as another PR opportunity need to be snubbed. The NITI Aayog itself is viewed more as a Government body. Instead it should be viewed as one of professionals or subject experts.

One clear result of this 'New Index Culture' is that states are focussing more on how they fare in the index rather than on performing or actually implementing schemes and making a difference to the lives of people. The Telangana State Government went to the extent of declaring itself the winner of its 'World Green City Award' in October 2022, by bringing out full page advertisements on the front pages of daily newspapers. The advertisement claimed that Telangana's World Green City Index considered Hyderabad, its capital city, as the winner, beating Paris, Montreal and Mexico City!

A Government self-proclaiming ad.

A new research outfit based in Patna, the Centre for Policy Analysis, came up with a 'Global Minority Index for 2022'. It is good that an Indian outfit took such an initiative. But it is not known, even within the country, for its data base on demographics or research on social fabric issues or for its field surveys. It gave India 'top rank' for 2022 out of 110 countries that it had claimed to cover for this index on 'religious inclusivity'. This initiative should have been preceded with an open discussion with a cross section of experts, instead of a political leader of the party in power suddenly releasing the report. The announcement of this index came in November 2022, in the wake of a US Commission ranking India under the 'threat' category, which India described as 'India bashing'. Within a few days, this Patna-based index was released. Subsequently, the US-based PEW Research published its survey indicating that India had become a 'discriminative' country more than ever before.

In April 2023 the IMF downgraded India's growth rate,

stating two reasons. One was 'slow domestic consumption' and the second reason was 'frequent revision in data'. While explaining, an IMF official in an interview to PTI on 22 April 2023, said that data revisions between 2019 and 2020 made the IMF change its assessment of India's economic growth trend. This insightful observation should remind us that this has also been one of the contributing reasons for India's poor ranking in different global indexes. This is against the background that the data released by the government is often described as 'provisional'. Quarterly data on growth, consumption, employment, etc., is often based on limited data and described as based on 'revised estimates'.

Reliability of data and its sources obviously is a critical input even for formulation of global indexes. But that has not led India to look into the status of its data and research sources. The government as a source for data is not always viewed as credible. This has not alerted the government to the significance of independent research and reliability of data. On the contrary, there has been a setback in the relevance and reliability of research and data. There have been no correctives and we continue to dent data in many different ways.

Recently, two seniormost officials involved with government data and its interpretation and assessment publicly disagreed about the authenticity of sample survey-based estimates. One, Pronob Sen, is a former chief statistician with an impressive record of heading the Statistical Commission; the other, Shamika Ravi, is a member of the PM's Economic Advisory Council. This newly constituted committee is expected to offer technical guidance for conducting surveys and better data framework and quality of data.

Both wrote in *The Indian Express* on July 7 and 8, 2023, contradicting each other. In this context, it is but natural to doubt the credibility of government data and claims. They create doubts about the credibility and reliability of the indicators of social and economic progress.

Yet another example of how vital data is called into doubt was in the public media in July 2023. The director of one of India's oldest and foremost research bodies was suspended, as its recent data findings on trends in social development were not in sync with the official stand. This body, IIPA, has been coordinating National Family Health Surveys (NFHS) credibly for decades. This institute has never before been caught up in controversy on any count over the decades, and its data is relied upon both in India and abroad.

The director, Dr K.S. James, was suspended on alleged irregularities in recruitment, although the faculty sources in the IIPA were quoted in the media, saying that it was on account of not coming up with 'positive data' that he was removed.

Some examples of this include data on open defecation, which did not match with the claims of the leaders in power. Also, more than 40 per cent of households were found to not have access to clean cooking fuel as claimed under the Government's Ujjwala Yojana. And also, that more than half of the population does not have access to LPG natural gas, as was being claimed by the Government. The Government did not bother about the credibility of its own premier research outfit. Earlier, Dr P.C. Mohanan, acting Chairman of the Statistical Commission and another other member resigned on account of similar 'inconvenient data'.

Data is being disrupted as though if there is no data, there is no problem; to manipulate data in order to suit or serve the powers. This outlook erodes the research scenario and potential within the government orbit and outside, depriving the country of its powers of research.

We seem to have ignored or forgotten the wisdom and insights of our early leaders. They had envisioned that data, research and evaluation services would be encouraged outside the government's orbit and that the more independent the research services, the more potential they have. Instead of downgrading the research potential of the country in different ways, it is time to promote rigor and respect for data, credibility of research institutes and research discipline among academics.

Happiness Index: What Did We Miss?

The King of Bhutan came up with the idea of Gross National Happiness (GNH) in 1972. He declared that this idea is more important than Gross Domestic Product (GDP). It is a holistic approach where equal importance is given to non-economic aspects which influence economic and social policy. Bhutan also created measurement tools that would be useful for policy making and for the GNH Index. These include both traditional areas of socio-economic concern such as living standards, health & education and less traditional aspects of culture and psychological well-being. The model includes nine domains like good governance, community vitality, cultural diversity and preservation of ecological resilience. The

Bhutan Government revised the formula in 2011 with 33 indicators. Even the UN adopted a Bhutan resolution in 2011 for a holistic approach towards 'development'. But in India we seem to have made no headway in this regard as if we lacked research support or policy direction and are confined to UN development indicators. What else explains the Planning Commission or its successor, the NITI Aayog, not developing an alternative and a holistic approach to 'development'? India has the advantage of unique cultures, heritage, a pro-Nature outlook. These were better articulated in our *slokas*, *satakas* and scriptures than our development policies.

The State Bank of India's Economic Division did better by taking on the 2023 World Happiness Index. It questioned India's position of 136 out of 146 countries. Questioning the criteria and based on the strength of 'social relationships' in India, it positioned India at 48 (instead of 136) and set a good example of looking at our own advantages.

Concern for Homogenising Research

Indexes should not be used to homogenise people, villages and the country. In the name of development, decentralisation should not be curbed. Distinct local characteristics should not be disrupted. Creativity, innovations and initiatives should be allowed and encouraged. Every region of the country is blessed with unique features and local peculiarities. Such identities should not be lost under the garb of policy. Research methodologies should not ignore local values and culture.

Research generally is put to use in a way to ensure that everybody consumes the same and acquires similar habits, to boost consumerism. This 'market compulsion' requires expansion of markets, and it serves the interests of the corporates, global manufactures and now even of political parties. Research policies in India should not promote such a trend.

Independent Research Sources Are a Better Bet

The way India is presented in different Global Indexes should be reviewed by a panel of subject experts in the country inside the Government and outside having some independent standing. This panel could even have Indian experts abroad. Such a panel should look into the appropriateness of indices and variables used, the methodology, sources of data, the experts relied upon and the relevance of sample surveys by each of the Global Indexes. If necessary, the panel could interact with those who are responsible for the index for further understanding.

In 2019, Abhijit Banerjee jointly won the Nobel Prize in economic sciences involving experimental research. His research has been to measure the effectiveness of government schemes in improving people's lives. He used randomised controlled trials as in medical research. He has been involved in research in many states under the banner of Abdul Latif Jameel Poverty Action Lab (J-PAL). He is an example of the kind of experts who could be invited to be part of an independent advisory panel. Earlier, the other Nobel Prize winner from India, Dr Amartya Sen, decades ago had even suggested an alternative to GDP-based measurement of development. Experimental research offers insights and much needed confidence for implementing massive programmes nationally. It would also improve performance levels.

Having missed an opportunity to formulate our own model of development when we were not as globally connected, we should not miss out again now to take the lead with our own research potential and our own development framework.

There is no evidence that an index improves performance at the micro level. But, the fact that the NITI Aayog has gone ahead and taken to ranking the states using the approach of global indexes, means that India has accepted index culture. The Performance Grading Index (PGI) by the Education Ministry with 70 indicators and 1000 points is another initiative which could be prompted globally. Of course, after correcting critical flaws regarding quality dimension of students being admitted, validating accuracy of data submitted by colleges to the Ministry and with validating measures built in.

Equally important and urgent is to reset the research scene in the country, and return national institutes to their pride of place. Leaving everything to one organisation, even if it is the NITI Aayog with its good number of experts, is not enough to steer the country onto a course of global leadership in the case of research, data gathering and analytics. This diversification of expertise, in fact, is also a prerequisite for global leadership in other fields or contexts.

Global Indexes Have Become a Toolkit for Global Activism

With penetration of Artificial Intelligence (AI), the global index scene is going to be a bigger psychological threat in the future. AI facilitates penetration of index culture beyond nation-states into domestic segments and will even erode regional strengths, unless India takes proactive initiatives. AI will further consolidate Indexes as part of the weaponry of the Big Powers. It should not be a surprise to learn that global superpowers and their institutes (corporate, economic and academic) are behind the proliferating global index culture. The Indian government will not be able to counter this trend on its own. Independent research power in the country should be encouraged to unleash its talents. India is blessed with knowledge and youth power to take initiatives towards such a pursuit. Academics should be encouraged to take on research in this regard on a continuing basis.

The fact that over two dozen global indexes have ranked India low year after year for over a decade shows that there is something missing in India's research paradigm. This is even more intriguing considering that India has the best of potential, experts and even impressive infrastructure. This situation calls for an overview of research in the country. Independent research and credible research institutes are critical. This book was written with the hope that India can correct, rejuvenate and reposition its research for a proactive global leadership role.

4

RESEARCH FOR GOOD GOVERNANCE

'The Emperor's New Clothes' View of Research

In the parable of the Emperor's New Clothes, the people surrounding the emperor tell him only what he wants to hear. In this sense, the 'emperor's mirror' confirms the emperor's view of himself. The news media is often criticised for becoming like the emperor's mirror. If research outfits too operate in this way, it signals a decline of democratic traditions, and the decay of the regime. Modern emperors seem to prefer a mirror to an X-ray, which exposes the undercurrents and reflects both pros and cons. This is when research becomes a third eye, seeing through the layers and unearthing the truth. The status of research in a country at various levels indicates the swings between the 'emperor's mirror' and an X-ray which points to the correctives and interventions required.

Independent Source of Public Opinion

Information flows and research findings from independent sources could save the emperor from going out naked. In a Parliamentary democracy, the significance of independent sources is even greater. We have good examples recently of a leader losing power for failing to take note of a vacuum in public perceptions, which independent research could have revealed. The classic case is Chandrababu Naidu losing power in 2019 as Chief Minister of Andhra Pradesh when he relied on news media and in-house opinion surveys conducted by sponsored agencies. Traditionally, news media and independent voices and research were prime sources that governments relied upon. Independent public opinion surveys on contentious issues continue to be used.

Successive governments failed to examine the global indexes depicting India in a poor light. As a result the government missed an opportunity to take them as an early warning and correct course.

There are instances of independent research saving political regimes from embarrassing situations. Indira Gandhi abruptly abandoned the Emergency in 1977 and unexpectedly declared general elections. This was prompted by the research findings of an independent researcher. Only noted columnist Khushwant Singh referred to this in his famous column 'With Malice Towards One and All' in the *Hindustan Times*. A more recent example is the Union Government withdrawing the three contentious farm bills in 2020, based on independent research. In the absence of institutionalization of independent research or decentralisation of administration, the government's tendency is to take the media's internal sources and 'instant public opinion surveys' as good enough to base decisions on.

For governance to become responsible and 'good', independent research is a pre-requisite. No government can claim to offer 'good governance' without allowing independent research. Out of 700 government schemes, only between 14-24 include some research, and this is not good enough. Recently it has become the practice to use research to support the scheme's claims or because of obligatory requirements (of auditors or donors).

If the free press is viewed as the 'fourth estate', independent research could be viewed as the 'third eye' of the government, saving them from embarrassment. Research enables a more responsive regime.

Instances of suppression of independent research, expecting it to toe the government line, reduces the credibility of research in the country, built over the decades. The case of CPR (Centre for Policy Research) in September 2022 is a good example. Its 50-year standing as a credible research-based think-tank has been dampened with Income Tax raids and wide coverage of the same in the news media.

Research in open societies is invariably conducted by multiple agencies of different origin and motivation. Some of these organisations are under Company Act, some are Trusts or Societies, many are also part of the government or under its control even if nominally autonomous.

Every 10 years, the Census is carried out to understand the size and composition of the Indian population. Its revelations remain—like a rainbow—for a short period. The periodic sample surveys by the NSSO (National Sample

Survey Organisation) make a similar transient mark. In the late 1960s, ORG (Operations Research Group) changed the marketing of consumer brands and retail distribution in the country with its monthly field research reports. Its survey in 1973 on child labour created a flutter and led to judicial intervention and a series of government initiatives. CSDS (Centre for the Study of Developing Societies) carries out election surveys which often change the political discourse, but this is largely during poll campaigns. CPR's periodic policy reviews have brought a new dimension to the framing of public policies. PRIYA has brought new enthusiasm and sensitivities among elected functionaries of Panchayats. Pratham's ASER (Annual Status of Education Report) has helped engender a concern with outcomes in school education. NFHS (National Family Health Survey) rounds have bought concern for social development parameters. ADR's (Association for Democratic Reforms) analysis of contesting candidates to the Election Commission brought a new perspective to elections, but sadly has made no lasting difference after a decade. CMS's study on election expenditure poll after poll and its annual track of the citizens' experience with corruption in availing of public services has shifted the focus in public discourse. CSE's periodic investigation reports and reviews are good examples of independent research. Sadly, the effect of much of this research is momentary and soon forgotten in the absence of any follow up, even by the concerned Ministries.

Promises, Claims and Performance

Back in 2014, the Prime Minister was quoted in the news media, repeating that 'by 2022, we should do one task. There should be nobody in the country who does not have a house, who is without water, electricity connection and toilet. This is the minimum task we should do.' But now as we are ushering in the 2024 polls, where do we stand on these and other such critical claims and promises? The same news media also reported that the new President of India's village in Orissa got electricity only after her nomination in mid-2022. The Jal Shakti Minister replied in the Rajya Sabha around the same time in 2022 that less than 52 per cent of rural dwellings had tap water supply. (Whether they could actually use the water in the house is different from having a water connection). Also, every village in some states was declared free of open defecation. The concerned Ministry even claimed so in the Parliament. The states are being rated every year for the last few years in this regard. But a 2021 survey by South Asia Labour Network found, based on its field survey, that '45 per cent of India's population was defecating in the open. It further reported that over 12 lakh toilets constructed do not exist.' This too was reported in some newspapers.

In 2016, the Prime Minister promised and reiterated that by 2022, farmers' income would double. This would have required a continuous double digit growth, against the reality of 2.8 per cent growth. Speaking in 2018, the PM said that, 'by 2022, my government will ensure that everyone has a house.' A noble promise indeed, but the latest government data paints a sorry picture. The PM Awas Yojana Dash Board states that over 60 lakh sanctioned houses, 50 per cent of the target, are not to be completed.

A July 2022 report of the Ministry of Statistics and Program Implementation revealed that cost overrun had increased from 13.4 to 22 percentage points between 2018 and 2022 in the case of 224 high volume projects, including the flagship programmes of the Union Government, against only 98 schemes in the previous year which suffered cost overrun. Why was there a cost overrun in such major national projects? It is yet another fallout of the government formulating schemes and implementing them without research or basic analysis on critical parameters, not conducting reliable monitoring and not allowing independent assessment of the project cycle.

For leaders, both promises and performance requires the backing of research. The larger the gap between the two, the greater is the need for research. Similarly, the greater the centralisation of governance, the greater the requirement for independent research.

Child Labour: Does It Exist?

Consider the fact that the Minister for Labour informed the Parliament Standing Committee in July 2022 that the only figures available for child labour were for 2011 and no data was available since then. He did not say that it was because the National Child Labour Project, which had been running for over three decades, had been merged in 2016 with the Samagra Shiksha Abhiyan. As a result, it is no longer clear whether the government is concerned with child labour in the country. This is despite the fact that the Parliamentary Committee in 2021 had given one year to the Ministry to update the data on child labour. This attitude is more than astonishing; it pains me personally. For I was part of the team at ORG, Baroda, in 1972-73 which on its own brought the phenomenon of child labour in the country to light and that first estimate which hit the national headlines was 41 million. It was to the credit of the judiciary that in a suo moto initiative it asked the government to explain the phenomenon. Even then, the government showed its ignorance and even tried to brush aside the research finding as of a 'private agency'. The government then was made to commit to conducting periodic surveys to establish the extent of child labour and do something about it. This was almost forty years ago. The Union Government took several initiatives to address the social problem and set up the National Child Labour Project. It also entrusted the responsibility of conducting research to the National Labour Institute, which had been coming up with data and research. To have no data implies that there is no concern. No research means no initiatives will be taken to address the situation. Child labour data was expected to be collected by 24 Union Ministries including the Home Ministry. In 2021-22 all these Ministries told the Parliamentary Committee that they did not have any data and claimed that the next Census, in 2021, was expected to come up with fresh data on the extent of child labour. 'Scarcity of funds and mechanism to find out the number of children engaged in child labour' was what the Ministry claimed, as if ignorant of the forty-year-long crusade in the country. This is despite the existence of a National Policy on Child Labour for 36 years, the Child Labour Protection and Regulation Act of 1986.

Farmer Suicides: Inconvenient Data

Governments have taken to ignoring or denying inconvenient data, even when it is in the public domain. Have farmer's suicides been increasing or decreasing over the recent years, given the claims of successive governments that they are taking initiatives to improve the situation of farmers? Even the National Crime Research Bureau (NCRB), who should be able to provide an answer, goes by what the government of the day wishes to project.

In July 2022, a Member of Parliament brought to the attention of the House a study by Punjab Agriculture University on farmer's suicides in Punjab in the previous 18 years. This study was sponsored by the Punjab State Government. It brought out that during the period from 2000 to 2018, 9291 farmers committed suicide in the districts sampled and there were 16,594 suicides state-wide during the same period. To this the Union Minister for Agriculture replied in Parliament that he was not aware of any such study by that University and, instead, quoted the NCRB figure of 1805 suicides for the same period. Obviously, the difference between the figures of two agencies is bound to keep the public confused and allow the state and the union governments to claim what they please.

The NCRB data uses different research methods to that of the Punjab Agriculture University study. The latter used household field surveys in sampled districts, whereas the NCRB relied on complaints registered in police stations about farmers deaths by concerned authorities in the district. It is well known that not all suicides are reported at the police station and not all those reported are counted and registered by the police. Even more, suicides of women in farmers' families are not considered as 'farmer's suicide'. It is not only the NCRB which does not consider women as farmers, even the Union Ministry does not.

This example reminds us that an independent agency doing research, even on such contentious issues, can be more credible. When a different set of figures is put out, it brings into question the reliability of government data. And a lack of credible data, even in such isolated instances, hampers initiatives by the government.

'Growth data', in fact, hides more than it reveals, as is well known to journalists who cover it prominently. And in the absence of reliable government data, civil society organisations like SOS, CSE, CMS and many others offer figures, even if symbolically. They even take action or relief measures.

Data on Manual Scavenging

Yet another example of the government denying itself reliable data is regarding manual scavenging, as if pushing the facts under the carpet is a better way to solve a problem. Even after 75 years of plans, claims and promises, manual scavenging continues because of the denial mode adopted by successive governments. The Union Government told Parliament in July 2022, for the second time in two years, that 'there has not been a single death due to manual scavenging' whereas the *Safai Karamchari Andolan* claimed 535 deaths in the last five years. In fact, two years ago when the news of the death in a sewer of a manual *Safai karamchari* two kilometres away from Parliament House broke, the Government denied in the Parliament that even a single death had occurred. The fact is that the government, in the form of the National Crime Records Bureau, had stopped recording any such deaths three years earlier in the wake of the much-publicised Swachh Bharat programme promising a toilet in every house. This is despite the fact that manual scavenging was banned in 1993 and made a punishable offence by an Act in 2013, which also provided for rehabilitation of such workers. Since then, District Collectors have been outsourcing the work, getting rid of the problem by not identifying a single case and avoiding compensation or rehabilitation as it is now a private contractor's problem.

'*Beti Bachao, Beti Padhao*' Campaign: Misplaced Priorities

The lack of research reminds us of the misplaced priorities in addressing critical long-standing problems of social development. Instead of understanding the scope and structure of deep-rooted issues through research, successive governments have taken the 'publicity approach'. Take for example, the '*Beti Bachao, Beti Padhao*' campaign. This campaign disregards the deep-rooted, misguided social values. To change these values requires research-based motivational community networking. No data has gone into this campaign in the last few years, nor is any outcome known as there was no effort to evaluate it, unlike in the case of the 'Swachh Bharat' campaign. Consider that between 2016 and 2018, Rs.446 crores were spent for the '*Beti Bachao, Beti Padhao*' campaign, but 78 per cent of that was spent only on media publicity. On this, even the Parliament Standing Committee expressed its regret in its report. No amount was budgeted for any research or data analysis or evaluation, even though such a scheme cannot be operational without research backup. And, in 2022, this '*Beti Bachao, Beti Padhao*' scheme was closed down so that there would be no more questions on it! Also, no need for any data, analysis or research.

Concern for Outcomes

Almost four decades ago, global agencies began to base their development lending and funding policies on outcomes. This was supposed to shift resource allocation based on results and outcomes in terms of real improvement to infrastructure, the environment and social empowerment. But this 'outcome-orientation' did not affect actual budget formulation until around two decades ago. As the shift would require considerable research and evaluation, that orientation never took off beyond the experimental stage. Today, with over 700 national schemes to do with development, including and social inclusion and equity policies, hardly two per cent of the projects can be said to come under this strategy. This further indicates the low status of data, research and evolution. It has also led to fudging or manipulation of field data to project favourable 'outcomes', depending upon the political claims of leaders. The performance of many schemes was never looked at from an outcome or impact perspective.

Although a few years ago the NITI Aayog and a few leaders in power claimed that the concern of the government had shifted to the 'outcome' of what is spent and budgeted for, there is no substantiated evidence of that shift. An outcome concern requires monitoring, measurement or evaluation of the difference that expenditure has made. While such an emphasis is much claimed, there are no examples of it being implemented or even experimented with. Instead, public discourse continues in terms of electoral promises, rhetoric, claims or budget allocations.

Self-help groups (SHGs) were formed formally as a national scheme in 2011, based on the recommendation of an Advisory Council to the Government, consisting of social researchers, as a part of the poverty alleviation and rural livelihood mission targeting women. Some 78 lac groups are claimed in the country, with several crores disbursed as loans to village women. So far there is no independent assessment of the scheme as to the extent to which the scheme has alleviated conditions for women despite the fact that loans increased by 45 per cent between 2017 and 2021, for example. One study, by the Institute of Rural Management in Anand in 2022, has not even been taken note of (as it implied that the programme in question had not made much difference), despite several implications for livelihood activities. The committee which recommended the scheme assumed that its implementation would be closely monitored and also evaluated periodically. Even after a decade there is no evidence of an independent study because the scheme is being continued as if it were a tool for political patronage, as pointed out by the independent study of the Institute in Anand.

Recognising the significance of outcome concern, the Cabinet Secretariat of the earlier government formed a high-level group consisting mostly of retired bureaucrats and a few outside experts (the Director General of CMS was one of them from 2010 to 2014). They were assigned to keep track of the performance of the Ministries. This experiment was never assessed or analysed. And once there was a change in the party in power, this independent effort to assess outcomes was given up by dissolving the committee specially formed for the purpose.

The outcome concern requires research at the outset of a scheme, monitoring of its implementation and analysis of the impact that the scheme has made compared to what was expected and claimed at the outset. Sadly, the way many of the schemes have been announced and passed in the Parliament or assemblies without debate or discussion during recent years does not allow outcome discipline beyond the rhetoric of the leaders.

There have been multiple schemes for 'women's empowerment' over the years, some initiated by the Union Government and some by the State Governments. Taken together, what has been the difference or outcome on the ground, in the communities, in families and individually? For example, banks were advised by the RBI recently (2022) to increase loans to women. The percentage of loans sanctioned has gone up from five to 21 per cent in 2022. How much of that sanctioned money was actually dispersed and how many women have actually utilised this scheme is not indicated by the banks or by any independent source. What was the basis for this four-fold increase in loans to women overnight and what was the expected outcome of these loans? Was it based on any research or analysis, and if so at what level, by whom and what are the lessons for the future? Or was it more on account of an impending election? My book, *What Empowerment of Women Should Be* (2023) in Telugu on women's empowerment, based on a case study of my village, examined the issue at the micro level.

Women's representation in policy-making legislatures has remained less then fifteen per cent in the last fifty years despite the many claims and promises of successive governments to increase it. Why has there been no research on the phenomenon, particularly after reservation was introduced in the panchayats, as if even that did not lead to an increase in the representation of women? Do political leaders and parties place such little value on their own promises? Consider that, although the number of women in the Lok Sabha during 1999-2019 was 236 against 2051 men, women MPs asked 1655 questions on agriculture against only 29 asked by male MPs. Even in the case of health, 1989 questions asked in Parliament were by women against 648 questions asked by men. Such an analysis of the data made available by the Parliament secretariat was never highlighted, as it does not suit political party bosses.

Denial of data is the easiest way out, but it amounts to pushing the problem under the carpet. Fiddling with figures compromises one's own credibility. This is not realised or perhaps it is actively ignored. Avoiding research is a form of denial by the leaders in government. Politicising data and research too imperils the government, and the country. The presence of truly independent research institutions could save the powers from embarassing situations, and from wasting its resources.

Of course, there are instances of availability of data collected by the NCRB and yet there have been no serious interventions either in policy making or in implementation. For example, the NCRB revealed that in 2021, rape cases increased by 19.3 per cent as compared to 2020 which amounts to 87 rape cases per day on average. Over all, crime against women in the country including rape increased by 13 per cent in 2021. And yet neither the news media, nor any of the many court cases including public interest litigations, referred to this data from the government's own source even at a time when a number of active citizens were fighting against the release of 11 people guilty of raping a woman and murdering seven members of her family including her three-year-old daughter. There was no Suo moto cognisance of the matter. All this brings out the fact that data matters only when it suits the government of the day, and when agencies are aware of it. This unfortunate phenomenon has not motivated any study or initiatives, particularly legislative ones, or correctives in implementation.

Another example of a gap in research concerns the proliferation of television channels, which exposed children to violence and led to a rise in deviant behaviours. The CMS Round table as early as 1990, inaugurated by I.K. Gujral, had deliberated on the (then) impending proliferation of television channels, particularly foreign channels, and their impact on children. This did not lead to further research, neither by the government agencies like the NCERT (National Council of Educational Research and Training) nor by any academic. Nor did the specially formed bodies like, for example the NCPCR (National Commission for the Protection of Child Rights) headed by Shanta Sinha, conduct any field research or analysis of data over the years.

Even now there has been no independent time-series study on the impact of social media or new gadgets including mobile phones on children. Yet another example involves the significant difference in education levels and the jobs market. Even in terms of skill empowering there are no serious long-term research studies at any level, or of the promises made to the public in this regard. Continuous failure to take on such social phenomena, by successive governments and academics, signals a decay in the concern for the future and lack of will to take course correctives. Thus the decline of data collection, research and evaluation engenders a vicious cycle of poor governance.

This overview suggests that governments are not anxious to avail of research tools and institutions which could bring in efficiency in the functioning of government schemes and help improve their credibility. Instead, governments are scared, suspicious of the potential of research, particularly independent research. This has cost the country, as the discussion of India's ranking in various Global Indexes showed.

Early Origins of Policy Research

The early origins of research in India can be traced to the Indian Institute of Science (IISc), Bangalore, founded in 1909. Although it pioneered fundamental science research, it helped set a certain discipline and baseline for social science research as well. Its early directors never lost their Indian moorings while building up the IISc as a world class institute with several pioneering research pursuits. Industrialists J.R.D. Tata, Vikram Sarabhai, T.A. Pai and V.K.R.V. Rao, in particular, need to be remembered for their vision.

Four-front Focus

Research received a four-front focus in the first fifteen years of independence. **First**, a definitive recognition of the significance of research as an essential component of nation building. **Second**, the setting up of research institutions to provide continuity. **Third**, the independent status of these institutions, so that research does not become subordinate to politics but retains its objective position. **Four**, assigning or recognising people of virtue to uphold the stature of research. This focus gave early directors of research bodies their professional calibre, with national concerns and foresight. It is what led to Indian research acquiring a wide range of infrastructure and worldwide recognition.

One of the early initiatives of the Planning Commission in 1953 was to constitute a 'Research Programmes Committee' to set an agenda for the research needed in support of the Five-Year-Plans. In 1958, based on the idea of scientific temper, the Parliament passed a 'scientific policy' resolution. A follow up to that in 1968 was a committee on social science research, with V.K.R.V. Rao as Chair. It was this committee which recommended the idea of an Indian Council of Social Science Research (ICSSR). In 1975, the spirit of scientific temper was even included as a part of the fundamental duties of the citizen, 'to develop scientific temper, humanism and spirit of enquiry'. A decade later, in 1987, the education policy reiterated the 'development of scientific temper'. And yet no significant turning point can be recalled to boost research thereafter. Until in 2018, when PM Modi surprised the country by reminding it about scientific temper and called on scientists to nurture it. Inaugurating the 105th Indian Science Congress at Imphal, the PM assured the nation of its 'rightful place among the frontline nations'. The PM's reiteration of the government's support to scientists, researchers and for the spirit of enquiry should have helped revive the importance of research. Though much was expected, the decline of research culture has seen no reversal ever since.

Policy research in India can be traced to Prasanta Chandra Mahalanobis. Starting with the Indian Statistical Institute and at the Planning Commission and its Programme Evaluation Organisation (PEO), he made a foundational contribution to research culture and infrastructure. G. Parthasarathy, J.P. Naik, pioneers of the Indian Council of Social Science Research (ICSSR); K.N. Raj, P.N. Dhar and N.P. Negi at the Delhi School of Economics; Rajni Kothari, founder of the Centre for the Study of Developing Societies (CSDS); the National Council for Education Research and Training (NCERT); Institute for Social and Economic Change (ISEC) in Bangalore set up by V.K.R.V. Rao; the Centre for Policy Research (1973) with Pai Panandikar as its president; Institute of Defence Studies and Analyses with K. Subramanyam, Durgabai Deshmukh, founder and Pradipto Roy as director of the Council for Social Development (CSD); Shanti Swarup Bhatnagar of the Council of Scientific & Industrial Research (CSIR); Indian Agricultural Research Institute (IARI); Indian Council for Research on International Economic Relations (ICRIER), these are some of the early pioneers of research in India. Then came the next wave of research outfits. These included the Indian Council for Economic Research (ICER), Tata Institute for Social Sciences in Bombay, and Tata Institute of Fundamental Research, Physical Research Laboratories (PRL), Ahmedabad. There were others under various Ministries, which were expected to further research studies. These included the National Institute of Community

Development in Mussoorie, the National Institute of Rural Development in Hyderabad, Indian Institute of Mass Communication, Indian Institute of Foreign Trade, Indian Institute of Public Administration, Indian Council of Medical Research (ICMR), National Institute of Health and Family Welfare (NIHFW, after merging institutes on Health Education and Administration and Research).

From outside the government, Vikram Sarabhai's role in setting up the Operations Research Group (ORG) in Baroda was a significant turning point in 1968. G. Parthasarathy, first vice chancellor and Prof B.D. Nagchaudhury of Jawaharlal Nehru University in New Delhi, deserve special mention for promoting research faculties and a research environment. Many other premier Universities added research as a discipline and also took up projects. The next wave of institutions which gave a fillip to research included the Delhi School of Economics and its offspring, the Institutes of Developmental Studies in Madras, Ahmedabad, Trivandrum and Lucknow and of course the Schools of Management and Indian Institutes of Technology (some of them with social science faculties). Potla Sen of the Administrative Staff College of India (ASCI) in Hyderabad took initiatives towards policy analysis and evaluation. The Gandhigram Institute of Development and Health was set up T.S. Soundaram Ramachandran near Madurai. The A.N. Sinha Institute in Patna took early research initiatives, mostly on economics and development.

Faculties of various disciplines have been involved and engaged in social science research. These include anthropology, sociology and social work, psychology, political science, economics, agriculture, economics and development studies, demographics and statistics, communication and social change and geography. Despite landmark studies by researchers like Radhakamal Mukerjee (Calcutta University), M.N. Srinivas (Mysore University), and S.C. Dube (Sagar University), Professor Damle (Pune University), and Dr T.N. Madan in the mid-1950s, social anthropological research never took root on its own or in convergence with other disciplines. Economic development remained focussed on poverty, employment, savings, expenditure, investments and agrarian issues. Sociology and social work diffused their concern despite glaring and urgent social development issues. Environment and ecology is a recent concern. None of these disciplines came up with their own basics and India-specific methodologies. Demographic studies remained focussed on population growth, family planning, migration and urbanisation. Overall the focus was on political and electoral issues, and on influence and persuasive aspects. Fundamental research on change, both economic and social, received disjointed interest. Even PEO, set up by the former Planning Commission did not take on impact studies as they were engaged more in monitoring. Social research has to be inter-disciplinary and multi-focal to make a difference.

The case of the Lal Bahadur Shastri National Academy of Administration in Mussoorie echoes the missed opportunities at the Indian Institute of Advanced Study in Shimla. Despite its involvement with policy analysis, it did not take the initiative to develop research methodologies and adapt them to the unique Indian scene. For example, one could have expected the Academy to engage in research on implementation of the Right to Information Act and the difference it has made in governance. The Administrative Staff College of India (ASCI) is another example with a difference. It received funding from the government and international agencies for several of its studies but its interests have been ad hoc and it has taken no proactive initiatives and longitudinal studies. What has been the fundamental difference these institutes have made to the research paradigm? None of these institutes has contributed to the evolution of India-centric research methodologies. Nor have they led the way in a program evaluation approach as some private outfits like ORG, CSDS and CSD have done. Most of these agencies today are going through a lull in their activities as if lacking support and direction.

Facilitative Factor

Decades ago while recommending the setting up of the ICSSR, V.K.R.V. Rao suggested that social science research is a 'facilitative factor for nation building' and 'social knowledge is important to promote and regulate social change and to produce a dynamic and healthy society'. He expected that 'social science research will have far more effective and continuing impact'. No leader in the government since has reiterated such a role for research in the last two decades.

ICSSR was constituted to promote social science research in the country both in academics and towards public policy. I had the benefit of interacting briefly, in Baroda in 1972-73, with J.P. Naik who had pioneered its operations as its first Member-Secretary. I also reviewed its operations at the instance of Professor M.L. Sondhi, its Chairman, in 1998. I am fortunate that I interacted with many of these pioneers. Over the years since, ICSSR has been organising workshops and training programmes in research methodologies through its sponsored institutes at different locations. More recently, ICSSR began sponsoring short programmes on research methodology through newer agencies like the Atal Bihari Vajpayee Institute. However, what difference these workshops made in consolidating social science research in the larger context of policy and programme evaluation was never reviewed, as each activity was viewed in isolation. Many of these institutes have been participating in conducting CSDS field surveys, but mostly in an electoral context, not on any public policy or social change or any of the basic issues before the country. In the absence of India-specific research and locally ingrained methodologies, foreign agencies, generally profit driven and market-oriented ones, have gained ground and have spread their methodologies.

ICSSR started with four affiliate institutes in early 1970, and that number had gone up to 27 by 1993. Hardly half a dozen of these 27 could be said to be viable even after 50 years, according to Professor Partha Chatterjee of the Centre for Studies of Social Sciences in Calcutta. That was why S.L. Rao (a former Director General of NCAER, the National Council of Applied Economic Research) had suggested the closure of some institutions and merger of some of them. He pointed out that most of its sponsored research was focussed on and limited to data collection. A review committee headded by Professor A. Vaidyanathan (the Director of the Madras Institute of Development Studies) in 2007 observed that 'social research is increasingly commercialised and driven by the interests of the sponsors as distinct from public interest. The ICSSR is unable to reverse that trend due to its organisational structure and lack of adequate resources. It never acquired capacities to accomplish its mission.' The ICSSR could not even put forward any data bases. V.K. Malhotra, member-secretary ICSSR (2019), expressed his concern over the performance of ICSSR institutes. In a review of ICSSR, Professor Anjan Mukherji of Jawaharlal Nehru University had lamented that social science researchers ignored their responsibility and accountability to society at large. Even privately funded social science research should go through public scrutiny 'if the findings are put in public media or even if the findings of such research have implications to the larger public.' None of these reviews by senior professionals of the country made any difference to the standing of ICSSR.

Initially the ICSSR institutes took up studies on gender, health and elections. But soon the election studies shifted from analysis of post-electoral trends to pre- and poll-time predictive surveys, which get hyped in the news media and have only temporary relevance. Professor M.V. Nadkarni of ISEC, Bangalore, cautioned against doctored research and its potential to vitiate public opinion.

None of the ICSSR institutes ever looked into the kind of role the mass media plays in economic and social change and development. Even the effects of television on children or on family systems or on leveling the playing field was never a concern of these institutes, even on an ad hoc basis. Is this because no funding was forthcoming?

Despite the fact that a senior functionary, the Vice-President of the ruling party, was the Chairman of the ICSSR from 2017-20, it has not become a nucleus of social science research in the country, nor was there any repositioning in its network. Earlier, when the chief of the UGC had become the chairman of ICSSR, it did not give any push to social science research faculties in some 300 universities, which are languishing for shortage of funding, faculties and facilities.

During the same period, private agencies like ORG in Vadodara had shown initiative both with regards to methodology and its utilisation. The Institute of Social Studies (set up in 1985) in New Delhi, and even the publication *Economic and Political Weekly* (EPW) contributed far more in promoting social science research in India than most ICSSR institutes put together. In fact, their contribution can said to be even more than what the University faculties did over the decades individually in furthering experimentation or critical engagement on interdisciplinary research methodologies.

There are some excellent examples of India-centric research methodologies being developed and used by private institutions. These include the social research experiments of Seva Mandir in Udaipur, the Barefoot School of Bunkar Roy in Tilonia in interior Rajasthan, CSDS, Grassroots Research and Advocacy Movement (GRAAM) in Mysore and Jamia Milia's Jamal Kidwai School. All of these are initiatives deserve much support to scale up their activities. These institutes are concerned with grassroots perspectives and voices, and each came up with unique methodologies. In 1975-76, Jamal Kidwai, former Secretary Ministry of Information and Broadcasting, and I wanted to adopt the Tilonia model and instruct 'barefoot researchers' at the Jamia Milia Centre for Communication Research (which later was named after Kidwai). I tried to revive that idea in 2012 by setting up the Institute of Communication and Convergence

Studies at Noida. As this was an entirely new approach, it did not appeal to parents or students and the institute had to be shut down in two years. Copy-cat courses attract more interest than anything new and experimental, particularly the research centric prototype development and module courses that I tried to teach at that institute. Ten years earlier, I did experiment with the idea of research as integrated into every course at Mudra Institute of Communication (MICA), Ahmedabad, initiated by myself and A.G. Krishnamurty of Mudra Advertising, along with Kiran Karnik and Pradeep Khandwalla, former Director of IIM, Ahmedabad, and Kartikeya Sarabhai. But since its prime concern was advertising and public relations, research-driven programs in the larger context could not be kept up as a key concern for long. However, MICA has continued as an academic institute as it is backed by a big corporate house.

Besides providing a base line, Census data has not contributed as much as the National Sample Survey (NSS) rounds, and more recently the National Family Health Survey reports (five rounds so far till 2021) have revived both analytical and evaluative studies. So have the annual ASER surveys carried out by Pratham. Much earlier, the first National Readership Survey (1972) and first National Family Planning Survey (1973) and the first National Survey on Child Labour and housing by ORG triggered large-scale social survey research at various levels and prompted public policy research in the country, which I spearheaded (1970-85). Then came foreign funding agencies and sponsors like the Ford Foundation, CIDA, USAID, UNICEF, Bill Gates Foundation, etc. (There are many others). They changed the course and priorities of social research in India.

Most market research outfits in the country today are fully owned or controlled by foreign corporates. The origins of many remain unknown, even today. However, it was an Indian organization (ORG) which developed a paradigm for market research, survey research, applied social research and supplied data month after month to private industry and the Ministries alike for three decades (1965-95). It introduced the idea of 'syndicated research' so that findings would not remain the monopoly of any one, methodology would be dynamic and transparent, and survey research became a serious source for primary data. Now control of all such organisations and the methodologies developed by them is foreign-owned, including the ones engaged in political and electoral studies.

In 1971, Professor Everett Rogers of Michigan University, who developed the 'diffusion of innovations' theory, and I visited a dozen research institutes across the country when Rogers concluded, based on discussions we had, that hardly twenty per cent of research conducted in the country was ever utilised or taken into account in any decision making at any level. I tried to update this estimate during Rajiv Gandhi's Prime Ministership as at that time research received some positioning. But that estimate on the use of research was only marginally bettered, within thirty per cent. I could recount several specific examples, but will mention only three here. In early 1980, I did a research project with ORG on the girls drop-out rate in Madhya Pradesh for the Union HRD Ministry. They did not see the connection between a lack of toilets and the girls' dropout rate. On finding that my report had a chapter on toilets, the Ministry found an excuse to dump the report itself. (A few years later the report was revived by UNICEF). A few years before the Commonwealth Games in India, CMS did a research project, also for the HRD Ministry, on the status of sports stadia in India. The research pointed, with specific examples, to how the stadia were being misused by local bodies. The Ministry shelved the report as it did not endorse any of its new initiatives. In 2016-17 the government commissioned CMS, after a lengthy process of competitive bidding, to do a field assessment of communication of toilet and sanitation initiatives in the states. CMS went all out to submit all the 29 reports within the allotted time. In the meanwhile the team in the Ministry had changed and that led to independent reports being put in cold storage, and another study was commissioned.

If ICSSR-sponsored research is similarly neglected over the years it would be even more disappointing. Governments have been anxious to disallow publication of many of these research reports. The exception in more recent years are field surveys in electoral contexts. Of even more concern is the fact that after decades of ICSSR initiatives, no data base exists on any of the social development issues which can be used by any others. None of this helps bolster the credibility of data and research.

The state of affairs with social research reflects in the credibility of data which in turn determines its utilisation. Firstly, when the numbers and percentages become yardsticks for change, development and performance, they need to be transparently validated as to source, structure and timeline. Basic data should have nothing to do with politics or the party in power or with periodic election rhetoric. And data should never be accused or doubted on those counts. Numbers become deceptive if they are not credible and evidence based. Media coverage should not be a factor leading to 'fixing' the data. Survey research used to be based on considered views and recall but today it is based on instant or 'top of the mind' recalls. Like instant news for news channels, data cannot be based only on perceptions. And like fake news, fake data and research is on the increase. Technology seems to be facilitating that trend. Instead of data we are now concerned with ratings, rankings and indexes. With frequently changing socio economic parameters, the structure of data needs to be transparent to remain relevant.

India is fortunate that it has researchers of all backgrounds: social, philosophical, spiritual, etc. Many of them, original thinkers, contributed significantly to their fields even before India become independent. Their ideas and propositions enriched global thinking and frameworks for the future. Prasanta Mahalanobis (statistics and research), M.N. Srinivas and S.C. Dube (anthropology), Radhakamal Mukherjee, Nirmal Kumar Bose (sociology), Amartya Sen, Jagdish Bhagwati (development economics), C.R. Rao (analytics), V.M. Dandekar and Tendulkar (poverty studies), Ashish Bose (demography), Pritish Nandi (Journalist and parliamentarian), L.C. Jain (industry analysis), Yogendra Yadav (political science); these are only a few among many who have set examples for original thinking in the last 50-70 years. They exemplify the interdisciplinary outlook and approach to research that India needs, and even offered models which many outside India adopted or took note of.

Dr P.C. Mahalanobis pioneered the primary databases required to frame public policies and welfare measures, which set standards for the global statistical system. The tools he and Dr C.R. Rao developed continue to be used all over the world. Even the United Nations sought his guidance. At the UN's Statistical Commission, Mahalanobis explained what he had set up in India when it launched its development growth path in the 1950s. He was inspired by those at the forefront of the freedom movement and philosophers of earlier eras.

Given our pioneering history, where are we in 2024? Have we come up with any new methodology to monitor, understand and appraise the changes, the process of development and evolving public policies?

Social science research received an initial impetus from the aforementioned stalwarts in different disciplines. Then a second wave of market research, demographic studies and rural development drove applied research on questions of poverty and inclusiveness. There were several researchers from different social science disciplines who gave a push to India specific research. But they were soon side-lined by the influx of foreign funding and foreign agencies.

Today there are few prominent researchers who have contributed to social science research or analysis, and engaged independently with an Indian or local issue. Economist Jean Dreze, political scientist Yogendra Yadav, and historian Ramachandra Guha are a few prominent thinkers who have set an example. But they are viewed as 'anti-establishment', ignoring the power of their arguments and initiatives as alternatives.

The competitive compulsions of the news media and their ownership structure have begun to shape public debates on research, use of data and the way the findings are reported and covered. The way the GDP rate is indicated by different agencies from time to time, varying even within a month, for example, causes confusion about GDP. Similarly, poverty levels are indicated as changing from time to time, varying employment rates are claimed by different agencies, and inflation rates are announced without explanation, all of which have complicated public perceptions about economic performance. Even more, it has dented the reliability of data originating from government sources. The estimates of people living in poverty, for example, range from 34 million to 373 million! Which of the five estimates should one take for the number of poor in the country?

Recently, the use of analytics has sharpened the potential of data and research. But what are the contexts in which analytical tools are developed and used? How are they used for public policy formulation? With so much data and research around, are the users or consumers more discriminative today? Are public functionaries and policy makers making better choices in the larger public interest? Are citizens more active or have they remained passive? Is that not what research is ultimately expected to do? Are we in a better position to independently and objectively measure effects and change, particularly social change, citizen empowerment, social justice? Are the methodologies facilitating the exploration of such concerns?

Researchers should never forget that they are first citizens of the country and that they have a social and ethical responsibility. Research should not become a tool for manipulative initiatives and individual interests. Persuasive strategies should never lose concern for grassroots and the interests of the poor, deprived, far off and those outside the power system. Social science research has not reached its full potential in the public domain. As a result, the research discipline has not flourished and carved out a niche. Most premier institutes were launched during the decade of 1965-75 at the initiative of the government leaders of the time. In the later decades, research did not become a sought-after input to sustain democracy and development. Research has not made social justice any better understood. The new economic policy brought a new use for research. Today, research has become a tool to explore the Indian markets.

There have been no corrective initiatives like the J-PAL project at Seva Mandir (Udaipur) or the Barefoot experiment (Tilonia) or the GRAAM (Mysore) idea in recent years to see that research helps policies, planning and strategies, as much it has helped marketing, advertising, and the corporates. Research has been reduced to number crunching for manipulation and influence with not much attention paid to conflict of interests. Independence, objectivity, transparency and inclusiveness as well as validation, which are essential features of research, have not been given their due importance.

Academic Research, Public Policy Perspective

The Tata Trust has been a key supporter of fundamental research in India in many different ways. It has helped set up institutions like the Indian Institute of Science in Bangalore over 80 years ago, which remains to date a pioneer not only in fundamental research in science and technology but also in policy research. The Tata Institute of Social Sciences (TISS) in Mumbai is another pioneer and over the last 60 years it has trained an army of researchers. These two institutes are only examples among many other ways in which the Tata Trust has been supporting research, both fundamental and policy. In 2018, the Tata Endowment of Rs 50 crore was set up at the Indian Institute of Technology, New Delhi, for a school of public policy. Under the guidance of the Department of Science and Technology (DST) of the Government of India, the Tatas set up five Centres for Policy Research. Over the years, senior bureaucrats have been sent for short-term courses in public policy institutes in the UK and USA. This should set an example for other corporates.

Centres of higher education, including universities, have traditionally been engaged in locally relevant research. This is apart from PhD theses or the requirements of post graduate level research. In 1960-62, as a part of my master's degree program, I undertook two research studies. One was a socio economic study of Harijanwada in my native village of Mudunuru in Andhra Pradesh. The second was a study of Asia's then largest Jaggery Cooperative Society of Farmers in Anakapalli, AP. Both these studies laid the foundation for my interest in research and for pursuing it as a career. These studies acquainted me with different research methodologies. The topics were chosen by me, out of my own interests, and the faculty in the University guided me in conducting these studies. That was the situation in academia 60 years ago.

In 2018, the Ministry of Human Resource Development (HRD), issued a directive to vice chancellors and directors of national institutes that PhD thesis topics should not be on 'irrelevant' subjects and should be on topics of 'national priorities'. This implied that the Ministry had become the nodal point for all academic research pursuits in the country. This directive cannot be ignored, as research fellowships can be withheld as a consequence. Considering the implications of this directive on the freedom of students to choose their topics of interest in consultation with the faculty, it made the news. It was criticised for curbing the right to choose research topics and that in turn lead to a crackdown on 'dissent' in academic campuses. As it was becoming a controversy, the Ministry issued a clarification that it did not have any intention 'to curb academic freedom'. But then it was not an isolated instance. Efforts to encourage certain preferences in research topics were there even before, although not as a policy. In 2016, Jawaharlal Nehru University (JNU) was reported to be discouraging research on Human Rights, Rights of Dalits and marginal communities. And even open seminars on campus on such themes were discouraged. Even in 2022 such directives were issued to vice chancellors of universities. What does this signal to the social science research environment?

From the 1960s till today, it is possible to observe changes in academic opportunities and environment and how the spillover of politics into research and academics has changed the priorities and culture of research. Amitabha Bhattacharya, a retired IAS officer, wrote in the *Hindustan Times* about the HRD Ministry's directive, that 'it was against the spirit of free enquiry and the guiding motive was political and [would] damage India's knowledge ecosystem.' He further wrote that 'this will amount to dictating ideas and is against critical thinking that engages with plurality of ideas.'

After years of neglect for Social Science Research, the Union Government came up in October 2018 with the idea of web portals to build a 'research ecosystem' in the educational system. The Government acknowledged that 'only by good research' could there be innovations, which are essential to sustain growth and productivity. The objective of the Government's Impactful Policy Research in Social Science (IMPRESS) is to identify and fund research proposals in the social sciences which have an impact on governance and society. ICSSR was made the implementing agency of this scheme. The scheme was allocated Rs.414 crores till March 2021, but there is no evidence of any of that being used on the ground.

Shifts in Objectives of Research

The scope of research in India has undergone considerable change over the recent decades. While some change is bound to be there in terms of priorities and methodologies, the predominant change has been induced by, and on account of the compulsions of the market, politics, governance and even media. A few such trends are discussed here briefly.

Public and state policy formulation and implementation was a primary concern of research, analysis, appraisal and evaluation during the early years of independence. The motivation was the fulfilment of core national concerns and setting targets for development plans. These included poverty, employment, inequalities, economic and social development issues. Slowly and steadily, with the growth of electoral politics, this concern changed to supportive research or endorsement research. Instead of identifying and addressing needs and aspirations, the focus of research has been to influence the electoral agenda and endorsement of government claims. The objective has become focussed on targets and selectivity, not the total population. That this approach has kept the country divided is either not being realised or is dismissed.

Using research for predetermined objectives has become the normal course of research of late. This mostly meant 'command and control' interests, so that the government of the day could be 'somehow managed' (this is what a Karnataka Minister confessed in private, caught on video in August 2022). This in turn has led to using research for persuasive purposes more than for motivating citizens and activating civic society to make it participative. The propaganda approach requires a different kind of research to the motivational approach. In propaganda, claims become the message (as numbers and slogans). Whereas motivation, self-realisation and active participation brings ownership and helps implementation of programs to realise larger goals. The research methodology too is different. Top of the mind or Yes-No type responses are good enough for supportive research.

Although the country needs a *Swadeshi* outlook, research methodologies are alien and continue to rely on image-prompting methodologies. That is why the entry of foreign research agencies has become so easy. The government itself has shown a preference for them. Until 1965 developmental initiatives were taken up on a pilot basis before being implemented nationally. The pilot requires research as an essential component and only after assessing the pilot is the scheme considered for national or state level rollout. The country being so vast, with varied climate, cultural and living habits and habitats, research at the outset and mid-course makes a significant difference in implementation and for accomplishing the outcomes. But when the goal becomes 'one India, one leader and one model', this homogenisation shapes the scope and intent of research. Despite insights from past research, we seem to proceed afresh every time as if we don't want to learn from the past. In such a situation, research and analysis becomes supportive. Evaluation and impact research is not welcomed, particularly if carried by independent research agencies which are transparent. Monitoring and subjective opinions from within are taken as good enough. Overall, research is undertaken more or primarily for image, public relations and publicity. As such, what is expected of research is only that it should match the designed outcome. Research is trapped in a vicious cycle starting with promises and claims and ending with supportive or endorsing research outcomes. In this process the scope of independent research becomes much reduced. No wonder that against this background, academic faculties are kept out or remain as bystanders. No social science faculty can claim to be engaged in any applied or even fundamental research. The victims in the process are the people of the country and its academic base.

With 'more government' becoming the modus operandi now (although 'less government' is claimed), the scope of research has changed. Interestingly, the multiplicity of government agencies has led to personality-centric operations across all levels. The cultish functioning of leaders in government has also changed the scope of research, making it less transparent. This expansion of government has also led to expansion of an anonymous research network and this has even changed the nature of research and the methodologies used. Despite new technologies of communication and application packages today, research has become constrained. The phenomenon of one India, one election, one leader, one market and similar ideas have also changed the very scope of research.

> What drives research today? It is not so much concern for good governance, equity, harmony, participatory democracy, concerns for the future and the like. Overall, four different type of compulsions drive the scope of research and its utilisation. These include 'market compulsions', primarily concern for costs, consumerism, market share, monopoly, maximising profits, etc. The second is 'political compulsions' which is mostly electoral considerations and winning strategies. The third is government priorities which include planned development, welfare schemes, involvement of citizens, etc. The fourth is media compulsions. Because of change in the very paradigm of news media of all kinds engaged in public affairs, we are witnessing a new order which in turn has changed the very scope of research and priorities.

Despite such shifts in trends and viability issues, a few research organisations have continued their independent functioning and retained their standing. How did these agencies stand out? What distinguishes them?

What An Independent Research Outfit Can Achieve

The Centre for Science Education and Public Affairs Centre have set good examples for what an independent research institution can accomplish. One of the best examples is CMS, whose research-based proactive initiatives stand out. Some examples of its work include the first social audit in the country based on CMS research in the context of the most sought-after public service during the period from 1980 to 2010. The idea of interactive public meetings with stakeholders of public policies and services was an outcome of that social audit experiment. CMS Vatavaran, based on its research insights, was a unique experiment which turned into an environmental action movement (2000-2020). CMS's annual assessment, based on elaborate research methodology, brought to light the corruption that a citizen encounters in availing of basic public services (1995-2020). The CMS estimate of election expenditure in general elections and landmark assembly elections, kept reminding the nation about 'note for vote' phenomena and similar poll time practices (1990-2019) and their implications for the representative character of elected legislatures.

Vatavaran festivals were held in 57 cities spread across 24 states. They were 2-4 days long sensitivity programmes. Over and above these, CMS held conferences, workshops, campaigns, symposia, round table meets with different stakeholders and the public. These were held in some 15 cities spread across 12 states, and apart from environment, wildlife, climate change, the topics included RTI implementation, road safety, media, gender and journalism.

CMS also held a series of national lectures at prominent public auditoriums in New Delhi and state capitals like Ahmedabad, Bangalore, Bhubaneswar, Bhopal, Lucknow, Hyderabad. These are unique examples of independent discourse on public policies and emerging trends and consequences as in the case of television programmes on women, children, news bulletins and lifestyles.

The national lecture series organised by CMS are unique. Never before had an independent research body ever organised public interaction with eminent people such as Dr Verghese Kurien, Dr Ilaben Bhatt, Dr M.S. Swaminathan, Dr Nandan Nilekani, Dr R.A. Mashelkar, and others. The themes included 'Challenges and Opportunities of the New Millennium' (1999-2000), 'Analysing and Envisioning India' (2012), and 'Challenges and Opportunities of the Twenty-first century'.

There are other examples of independent research and initiatives. It was Durgabai Deshmukh's book, *Social Welfare in India* published in 1958-59 which led to many policy initiatives and the launch of women's development schemes in the following decade. No comparable study or book can be named as responsible for any of the policies in the last two or three decades. As independent outfits, the reports of ADR and ASER over the last decade have several pointers for policy and proactive initiatives. But, sadly, they remain in the news for a day or two, with no resultant policy intervention.

Research Could Improve Options and Future Prospects

The lack of research backup for the country's key policy formulations and their implementation is obvious today.

Even budgetary provision for research is no longer binding. The lack of research on many social policies and outcome indicators is costing the nation in many different ways. These costs are in the extent of delays, the wastage of talent, the underutilisation of resources, many policies failing to benefit the intended recipients, misuse of precious time, increase in discontentment, and the increasingly political view of development and governance. This has created a situation which allows political leaders and political parties to engage in 'accusation rhetoric' against each other and get away with all kinds of promises and freebies. This scenario also suits the news media, as hostile political parties are pitted against each other to generate viewership. If public discourse is to be logical more than emotional as it has become, research culture has to acquire its own standing.

For example, have employment opportunities in the country increased or declined recently? One could argue endlessly both ways, showcasing data as it suits the politically inclined arguments. Have crime rates in the country increased or decreased during recent years? Political leaders can generate a controversy every week, tossing out some data or other especially if that means diverting public attention from a more serious, logical and urgent issue. Even controversies inside the legislatures are sustained in animated debates, which take the country nowhere and the larger public remains gullible and passive. All this despite the fact that there is extensive research on jobs, employment, unemployment and that some flagship schemes, including MNREGS, were based on field monitoring and research by independent researchers or autonomous institutes. Despite the plethora of research, there continues to be uncertainty around the issues to do with poverty, jobs and employment.

Another example, in which I was personally involved, was in the early 1970s. The percentage of women participating in the work force, as reported in the Census of 1931, 1951, 1961 and 1971, varied widely. The percentage points varied between 32, 23, 28 and 12, respectively between 1931 and 1971. The percentage of working men was between 61 and 53 during the same period. Even in the 2001 Census, participation of women was 26 per cent against 52 per cent of men. Why was this so? What can be made of such unequal numbers? When I was at ORG I went to the Census officials in the Home Ministry to find out whether the questions asked in the household enquiry schedule varied. I found that it was the way the questions were prepared in the Census questionnaire which suppressed the role of women in general and determined the kind of budgetary allocations to schemes for women in particular. This data continued to mislead public policy formulation even after 1961, and the importance given to women and children in the Five-Year plans and annual budgets remained low. What was surprising was that this data from the Census was never looked into by the demographers or academicians of that time as they were part of one or the other establishment institutes. This distortion continued even thereafter.

Another example relates to forest cover in the country. By changing the definition or base line, the Government can claim whatever suits it. That is how Governments have been able to show whatever they wish, notwithstanding the actual ground situation even if there is independent research showing otherwise (for example, the CSE annual report). The government has been claiming an increase in 'forest cover' by including what is planted as a part of a campaign, not naturally grown clusters, as the global norm is. For example, *The Hindu* on September 12, 2022, reported prominently how forests are on the decline. The Government, on the other hand, claimed that there had been an increase in forest coverage. What is the net result of such contradictory data in the public domain?

Consumption trends are another example. To justify the claim that the economy is booming, consumption must be seen to increase. Through this, the government can claim that there has been an increase in employment. That is how consumption levels are claimed to be increasing and also therefore jobs, irrespective of ground realities. Any conflicting data by sources other than the Government are ignored or debunked. Sometimes the Government prompts agencies like FICCI or CII to come up with supportive data as in 2019, for example, as it was election time and the considerations were political gain, rather than the reliability and reflective nature of data. Similarly, to show that they have created an increase in employment, governments claim numbers of new jobs when the true situation is otherwise and the government's claims cannot be substantiated with reliable data. Often, the government makes the concerned State agency stop giving data or merges the data with something else.

This pattern can be seen in claims relating to literacy levels too. There are more than one third of people in some sections of the population who have never been to school. The school dropout rate too has been on the increase, particularly for girls. This obviously implies that several government initiatives have not made the level of difference that the government claims. And this cannot be tracked and corrected easily. When an independent ASER study brings out reliable data, which the government itself had endorsed (when it suited), it is ignored or another agency is asked to come up with another set of figures that suit the government.

A further example relates to corruption levels in public services. Governments tend to claim a decline in corruption in the country during their tenure because of their initiatives. And yet on the ground, the reality and experience of citizens is different. All governments tend to fudge data in different ways to show low corruption levels during their term. Corruption itself remains a routine practice and the problem is pushed under the carpet. The government either keeps quiet or gets upset when a global ranking shows India as riddled with corruption. On the other hand, if a well-known independent agency comes up with data on corruption in specific terms and in such away that it could be addressed at different levels based on reliable field research, the government is uninterested. Opposition political parties in a state tend to take such independent research more seriously, largely for electoral gain. The actual corruption becomes the problem of the 'other' and carries on.

'Unity in diversity' has been a slogan in the country for decades. When applied to development, it gives rise to different models in terms of empowerment or inclusiveness criteria in some regions and for certain sections of population. A prominent example of a distinct development model is Kerala. Himachal Pradesh is not referred to so much for its distinct model. So many research studies have been conducted on different models of development by the government, independent institutes and international research agencies. All of them have indicated the differing status of women, extent of citizen participation and how different periods have seen different patterns of inclusiveness. There is also the BIMARU proposition by Ashish Bose, based on demographic trends. However, there is no analysis comparing these different models and the extent to which research has contributed to improvement. Despite distinct differences in levels of development and the continuing ground realities in the case of Scheduled Castes, Backwards Castes and tribal pockets, there is no comprehensive research to find a way to improve their situation.

Similarly, despite reservations in local body elections for women panchayat members more than three decades ago, what difference has been made and what is the visible result over the years? Do we find an increase in active women in the forefront in any respect over these three decades? Do we find that women's participation has increased in decision-making roles? Have women's empowerment policies and programmes made the big difference that is claimed? The answer is, we do not know. The situation in the case of the environment or child labour is similar. Hardly any independent research exists on any of these issues even when these issues are continuing ones.

Why the Girl's Dropout Rate Has Hardly Declined Despite So Many Schemes

Each of the five National Family Health Survey (NFHS) reports in the last 25 years signalled many social development concerns. There has been hardly any definitive follow up research or analysis by any of the demographic Centres or Government agencies or academics that has been shared with the public. These reports are the result of coordinated research by the Institute of Population Science, Bombay, under the Union Ministry of Health and Family Welfare. It is the foremost autonomous institute in Asia on demographic studies. Their reports are considered official government documents.

PEW Research Centre is a Washington-based outfit that undertakes research on a wide range of topics. Its studies on India recently have been getting wide news media coverage as a 'global authority', although no Indian expert or specialised agency is associated with the studies of Pew Centre. What is the impression that this gives the world, and even within India? It implies that no such research exists in India, by any of the research agencies. For example, in mid-September 2022, Pew's report using 'government data' reported that nine million girls were missing, attributed to female foeticide in India during 2000-2019. Of them 7.8 million were claimed as Hindus. They analysed the data from the last three rounds of NFHS, including the fifth round in 2019-2020. There is no Indian demographer associated with this Pew Centre study or any collaboration with any Indian demographic centre, although we have had more than a dozen such Centres for two or more decades. India has banned prenatal sex determination testing (the preconception and prenatal diagnostic techniques) by an Act of 1994. This Pew study reminds us of the clandestine use of ultrasound facilities in India. This also means that the male-female ratio in the general population becomes skewed in favour of males. This analysis also signals sex related violence, crime and trafficking of women. The question is, why does the NFHS data not provide a direct estimate of the number of girls missing as a result of sex selective abortions? Even earlier, in 2010, a German non-profit research institute, the Institute for Labour Economics, had estimated the number of 'missing girls' in India during 1995-2005. This report had stated that 0.48 million girls per annum were selectively aborted during those ten years. What initiative have we taken to address these 'revelations'?

Consider another example of how data is ignored even when it is from an authentic independent source, perhaps because it suits neither the political bosses nor the news media. Based on his research, Dr T.V. Ramachandran of the Indian Institute of Science, Bangalore, revealed in September 2022 that in Bangalore there has been a 1055 per cent increase in paved surfaces over fifty years, with over 88 per cent decline in vegetation cover and 79 per cent decline in water bodies. Private surveys have indicated that the number of slums in Bangalore are four times more than what the municipal authority has put out. Yet this 'Bangalore drowning data' has not instigated any serious remedial measures.

5

RESEARCH INFRASTRUCTURE

Research Infrastructure in the Country

Never before has India's research potential and capabilities been as elaborate, extensive and impressive as today (2024). It is as a result of its research infrastructure, including institutes and experts, that India has a global standing in many fields. We are a key global player in space and satellites, defence arsenal, pharma, engineering industry and analytics and software and sciences. In all these, research plays a key role. Even market research, consumer behaviour research and public services and social research has helped that process. ISRO, DRDO, DRDL, NSTL, ICAR, CSIR, ICMR, the IITs, IIMs, etc. and a range of research labs have been pioneers of research while being under the government system. The same cannot be said in the case of government support to social sector research. Despite a number of global research players dabbling in the social sector, there is a dearth and even decline in social sector and policy research.

The Government patronage for research and development

has been extensive and goes beyond annual grant giving and budgetary provision. R&D efforts involving laboratories and institutes to do with defence, electronics, industry and science in particular have been visible. That they were not linked with academic infrastructure is a different point. But the foresight that research should be decentralised in the country is evident from the fact that ICAR has more than a hundred institutions spread across the country, CSIR has more than 35, and DST, DBT and ICAR each has more than a dozen regional institutions with a number of initiatives in the earlier decades. This aspect deserves to be noted.

During the early period of independence, we were able to overcome various problems like drought, floods, shortages, external threats, etc. That process was facilitated by data, feedback, analysis, evaluation and field research. A retrospective review of India's great strides confirms the contribution of policy and social research. But it is not talked about or acknowledged anywhere in the country formally. This book is a small effort in that direction.

Five Phases of Research Infrastructure

As a part of the government's initial efforts, new organisations like the National Sample Survey and Programme Evaluation Organisation were created as a part of planned development. The faculties of the Delhi School of Economics (set up in 1950) and development research hubs around the country were sounding boards for social policy.

The next phase (1950-60) saw the creation of a series of National Institutes like the Indian Council of Agriculture Research, National Council of Educational Research &

Training and the Indian Statistical Institute. In the third phase (1960-75), Institutes were set up by Ministries to provide research and training support. The fourth phase consisted of a range of outfits outside the government to cater to the needs of the country in different sectors including industry and markets. A fifth phase was driven mostly by global or multinational interests after the 1991 reforms which brought about the liberalisation of the economy. This led to a boom in private consultancy firms. By 1975 India had a series of Institutes devoted to 'development', in Ahmedabad, Bangalore, Calcutta, Bombay, Hyderabad, Lucknow, Shimla, Patna, Chennai, Trivandrum, Bhopal, Bhubaneshwar and Chandigarh.

Within 17 years of independence, in 1963, India was able to launch a rocket into space by transporting it on a bullock cart, because the first step had been taken, of setting up National bodies for research in science, space, automatic energy, defence, industry, etc.

The Indian Institute of Science, Bangalore, Tata Institute of Fundamental Research, Indian Statistical Institute, National Physical Research Laboratory, etc. provided the lead in sourcing data, including for finalising the First Five-Year Plan. NSS, CSO, PEO were set up for estimating basic needs of the country. These agencies and their services offered correctives and confidence. The Green Revolution (1960-67), the name given to research-driven intensive agriculture, helped increase food production. That research and training from 66 Institutes of Agriculture Sciences helped achieve that early success is well known. The insights from this phase led to the setting up of research capabilities and infrastructure by way of institutions and experimental research and extension centres.

The next round of institutes with research portfolios were set up to focus on poverty, social divides, labour, gender, unemployment, rural development, social welfare, media and communication, child development, demography and primary education. The National Institute of Community Development (changed later to Rural Development, NIRD), NCAER, IIMC, NIPCD, NIHFW, etc. were set up. The main focus was on poverty, though employment, productivity, diffusion of innovations and behavioural change were also examined. When Union Ministries realised that they needed research and training support, most Ministries set up institutions to cater to their core concerns by providing data bases, research, and training. Realising that functional freedom would be better from outside the Ministry, institutes were setup as 'autonomous societies' with the concerned Ministry exercising control. Initially there was enthusiasm to conduct research, evaluate performance with feedback, training, and impact studies. Tribal Research Institutes were set up in states with considerable tribal populations.

Realising the implications of population growth trends across the country, Population Research Centres were set up between 1958 and 1972 in most states, mostly on academic campuses with the hope that they would induct young postgraduates into demographic studies. There are more than 20 population Centres in the country. The one in Sagar was the last one to be established, in 1999.

Dr Ashish Bose had come up with the BIMARU acronym in 1980-83 based on extensive research in the country. This refers to the states of Bihar, Madhya Pradesh, Rajasthan and Uttar Pradesh, which lagged behind in several development parameters. This idea was taken up not only by Prime Minister Rajiv Gandhi but many regional and local leaders. Doyen of industry J.R.D. Tata set up research bodies. The Ford Foundation, Rockefeller Foundation, and the Bill and Melinda Gates Foundation, international agencies like the World Bank, ADB, IDA, USAD, DFID all become major funders of research in India. The improvement in demographics in the country including Bihar, UP, MP, Rajasthan and Orissa over the next few decades was because of the momentum provided by research. *India 2021*, published in 1983 and edited by me at ORG, outlined the support needed to fill development gaps and inequalities.

In a key initiative, the Ministry of Education constituted ICSSR, the Indian Council of Social Science Research in 1971 with the hope of promoting social and applied research in different fields of development. It also recognised certain institutions and supported them financially. Apart from reimbursing salaries for the core faculty of those institutions, certain research projects were funded and training in research methodology courses was promoted. Ten of those institutes were established before 1972. Only three have been recently established, before 2010. At one point around 36 institutes were supported by ICSSR. In 2022 that number dwindled to 29. All of them were registered as non-profit societies. Most (more than 85 percent) of the funding given by ICSSR has gone into administration and establishment costs. A decade earlier in 2011, an ICSSR review pointed out that there were only 'six active players' conducting social science research in India. That was the first signal of the decline of social research in India. Few measures have been taken since then to refurbish research, until 2020 when the National Education Policy indicated certain proposals presumably to revamp research in the country. But none of these have made any difference in the last couple of years.

On the academic front, research methodology courses were added at the post graduate level, with a field research-based thesis as a course requirement. This was expected to nurture the research infrastructure in the country.

Even before independence, India had industrial research establishments. The National Physical Lab and the National Chemical Lab, for example, were set up before 1950. The Central Road Research Institute was set up in 1952. Today there are 44 research facilities on different subjects under the Council for Social and Industrial Research (CSIR). Only four of them were established after 2000. The last one was established in 2010, in Pune. The 44 CSIR research labs have had no notable outcome recently. PM Modi even presided over the annual CSIR meet in October 2022 and expressed his concern about their functioning.

On technology infrastructure also, India did not lag behind. In terms of utilisation of newer gadgets, however, a huge gap persists between regions and sections of population. Despite the proliferation of gadgets today, we are far from availing uniformly of the facilities and increasing access. The situation is governed by market forces rather than the government. Research should have been the first beneficiary of newer communication technologies and networks. Although telephone interviews, tele conferencing and digitalisation has helped data gathering, analysis and analytics, primary enquiry-based research has not changed so much, nor have the validation or reliability aspects of research increased.

Although there were more than 1000 universities (half of them private) and 40,000 colleges in 2022, India has remained far behind global educational benchmarks, particularly courses on research. Hardly half of them have a social science department. More than 30,000 PhDs come out annually in different disciplines including sciences, which is more than most countries including the USA. But this number far outstrips local demand. Hardly one third of this number find suitable employment in the country and many seek opportunities abroad. Many of those who have gone out of the country have made a mark globally as innovators or inventors and researchers. 70 per cent of the patents shown in India belong to NRIs. Holders of PhD degrees are expected to add to the potential of independent research. But they do not seem to have added to the momentum for independent research in the country.

The National Education Policy (NEP 2020) outlined a research ecosystem for the country. Never before had such a policy on research been enunciated in any of our national education policies. The NEP 2020 provided for a National Research Foundation (NRF), presumably to consolidate research endeavours in the country and as part of an attempt to revamp the education system in the country. The NRF is expected to help build research capabilities across academic subjects and consolidate research to meet the needs of the ministries in a pooled way. This initiative was meant to boost 'research culture' in the country. But in July 2023 the Union Cabinet decided to bring NRF under the government through an Act. Although NRF is described as a funding agency, it is also the approval and evaluating agency of research projects, and in charge of granting fellowships. The funding indicated in the Cabinet note—of Rs 50,000 crores—was mostly from industry, international agencies and others. The NRF Bill subsumes a 2008 Act (Science and Engineering Research Board Act) so that research activities at all levels in the academics, industry and outside come under the control and command of the PM directly or through the PM's Principle Scientific Advisor. So, in effect, the government—or, more specifically, the PM's office—wants to have control on research outside the government too! The scope and structure of NRF clearly requires a relook so that research acquires independence and credibility.

Although the New Education Policy of 2020 made impressive references to promoting research, there have been no follow up initiatives in the last couple of years. On the contrary, the post–NEP scene is one of predominantly supportive or endorsement research in the country, not independent research. On December 8, 2022, the Union Minister told the Lok Sabha that the Azad National Fellowships for PhD and MPhil which had existed since 2006 were to be discontinued based on recommendations of the Sachar Committee. Sukhdeo Thorat, a former Chairman of the UGC, pointed out that this withdrawal of scholarships meant depriving youth from minority communities of the opportunity to attend higher educational institutes.

While the NEP should be appreciated for its concern for the status of research in India and for recommending a National Research Foundation, the organisational structure of the NRF as provided for by the Union Cabinet in 2023 does not guarantee that it will serve its intended purpose.

In fact, t has been registered as a 'society' and filled with political Ministers and bureaucrats. Lessons have clearly not been taken from most of the similarly established societies in the country over the decades, which have neither enjoyed professional independence nor the privilege of initiatives. Those institutions are languishing. The NRF should not end up functioning in a similar way, particularly because the NRF will be under the direct control of the PM's office. The Bill proposes to raise funds from industry, international agencies and even philanthropic institutes. Only Rs.14,000 crores out of Rs.50,000 crores (for five years) indicated in the Bill (up to 2030) is from the Union Government, and the remaining from outside sources. Thus the claim that the Government is increasing allocations for research includes what is likely to be spent by outside sources. How such an arrangement will acquire professional independence, credibility, long range perspective and global competency, needs to be seen.

While it is good that the NRF has legislative backup, collaborative and multidisciplinary research in academics is not evident even in terms of budgets and allocations. The Bill is not explicit on strengthening research on social science, public policy and governance. On funding, the NRF does not specifically indicate support to social science and humanities research or to the nodal agencies like ICSSR. The commitment of funding to these institutes should be explicit. Funding for research in the academic institutions should consider the significant increase in the number of PhD candidates over the years and the research which leads to patents. The private universities too should be obligated to provide for research faculties and funding for scholarships.

There are nearly 250 institutes in the country focussing on research in the hard sciences: chemical, physical, earth, biological, pharma/medical, agriculture, engineering, forestry, etc. This contrasts with hardly 75-80 institutes focussing on social science, behavioural, economic and development studies. No new institute has come up in the last 15-20 years; most of them are 40-60 years old. Most of them are going through a difficult time either because of budgetary issues or lack of professional staff, guidance and encouragement.

Most research apparatus in the country is under government control or patronage and, in terms of numbers, it is impressive. Sadly, in terms of role, outcome and utilisation of these institutes, it is neither impressive nor uniform. However, past accomplishments have been impressive, and have measured against global standards. That is how many high-tech, managerial and marketing corporates the in US are headed by those of Indian origin, educated in India. And yet little importance is given to the contribution of research and its potential to make India a critical player at home and abroad. That not a single new research institute has come up in the country in any of the social science disciplines in the last decade is difficult to understand.

There has been no effort in recent years to review the status of the research apparatus and institutes of the country, together or individually or sector-wise. Since most of the institutes referred to here are part of the government or under direct or indirect control of a Ministry, there is no way to note how much of their research could be viewed as 'independent' and objective. Earlier, ICSSR operations were reviewed by senior professionals periodically. Perhaps not every activity of these institutes needs to be independent nor is that necessarily desirable. But globally, distinct credibility is attributed to independent research and the outcome of independent institutes. This is one disadvantage that India has now. The independent stature, free of the Government's control, of most research outfits has declined.

The research apparatus of a country need not be limited to the Government or rely on its support. Research by private agencies has far more potential. Also, their overall share has been on the increase in recent years, particularly since the 1990 economic reforms. Broadly, these non-government research outfits have foreign links at three levels. First, the research conducted or sponsored by the UN and associated agencies like UNICEF, UNIDO, Ford Foundation, USAID. Second, the research conducted or sponsored by foreign corporates. Third, the research by private corporate players serving the interests of industry, advertising and various lobbies. Industries, individually or together, sponsor research or get it commissioned by various associations like Chambers, Federations, Councils, etc. Research conducted by independent research agencies on their own does not serve the objectives of industry and the market.

Election Surveys: In the last decade, election time surveys have become the preoccupation of leaders, research agencies and the news media. Many such agencies have mushroomed. I have seen over thirty years how their surveys have proliferated, polluted the political discourse and helped the electoral process to become manipulative.

Their preoccupation with poll studies has led to a situation where what matters is what appears in the public media, and media projections in turn influence who wins or loses in elections. Neither planning, implementation, effects or concerns for the future are on the agenda of researchers and research institutes, both in the public and private space. Neither have these studies sensitised voters nor have they contributed to bettering governance in the country. But monetary support is forthcoming for such research far more easily.

There are several apex or nodal agencies that promote research coordination and funding of other institutes like ICMR, CSIR, ICAR, NCERT, etc. There are also some similar bodies outside the government. These include, for example, Market Research Association of India, Indian Sugar Mills Association, and the like. They have set certain standards and contributed over the years to data collection.

The presence of many global research agencies in India after 1991 has not helped the country improve its standing in terms research, evaluation and faring better on global indexes and competitive ratings. This is perhaps because the foreign research agencies with their multinational presence were more interested in securing 'consultancy assignments'. In government files, their services are described as PSU or project support unit, justifying their continued preferential role.

Tribal Research Institutes: There are 25 Tribal Research Institutes in the country, some of which have been in existence since 1952-55, some from 2016-18. A few of the state level ones are known as Tribal Research and Training Institutes, a couple of them as Tribal Cultural Research &

Training Institute (West Bengal, Telangana); all others are Tribal Research Institutes and most of them operate as a government department. Their main objective was to carry out research, promote development, identify the needs and problems, and conduct evaluation and ethnographic studies among the tribal population. The activities of these institutes are limited to occasional seminars, publishing newsletters and documentation centres and libraries.

Perhaps no other example is required to conclude that official 'research' is only in name. There is hardly any basic or applied or operational research in these tribal research institutes despite the existence of most of them for well over 50 years. There is no indication that any of the policies or programmes or development interventions over the years have been based on any research at these institutes, despite the fact that the union government has allocated budgets year after year. Half of the sanctioned posts in many of these TRIs were vacant as of January 2019, according to data given in the Rajya Sabha. An outlay of Rs 100 crore was made for these TRIs in the 2018-19 budget, for example. There is no outcome concern for this expenditure.

The idea of tribal research institutes came from the pioneers of India who realised at the very outset that we need to study and pay special attention to tribal culture and to their special needs. Some of these institutes were initially independent and then they were brought under a government department. A few were attached to a local university with the hope of generating research methodologies for anthropological research. But, overall, despite their long standing there is not much that has come out of these institutes. Most of them use research methodologies developed elsewhere. ICSSR has not made any special effort to initiate policy studies or develop appropriate research methodologies specific to tribal pockets and populations.

Even the creation of a separate Union Ministry of Tribal Affairs in 1999, for a focussed approach to tribal development, has not galvanised these TRIs. But in 2019, the Ministry announced four new TRIs and indicated plans to launch a National Level Tribal Research Institute to coordinate the activities of state level tribal research institutes and take up national level studies. There has been no indication of anything happening in that direction since then.

The four tables on the next page indicate the number of research institutes that have come up in the country over the decades with special reference to social, tribal, demographic and industry research.

Impact Studies (1975-1985)

The ISRO Space Application Centre, Ahmedabad, is a model for evaluative research as an inbuilt component of the SITE (Satellite Instructional Television Experiment, 1975). This was a global initiative in using satellites to reach out to six states in three clusters in five different languages simultaneously with the same video. As head of social impact research, anthropologist Dr Binod C. Agrawal had conducted a study in all these states concurrently over a period of 3-4 years. He was responsible for using sociological and anthropological research methods to study and assess specially devised television programmes on education, integration, health and community development. The uniqueness of this model was that it facilitated mid-course corrections, evaluated the efficacy and also offered insights into impact and training opportunities in the process.

ICSSR Sponsored and Recognised Research Institutes

Sl. No.	Name of the Institutes	States	Website URLs	Est. Year
1	Institute for Social and Economic Change (ISEC)	Karnataka	http://www.isec.ac.in	1972
2	Centre for Development Studies (CDS)	Kerala	http://www.cds.ac.in	1971
3	Centre for Studies in Social Sciences (CSSS)	West Bengal	http://www.cssscal.org	1969
4	A.N. Sinha Institute of Social Studies (ANSISS)	Bihar	http://www.ansiss.in/	1964
5	Institute of Public Enterprise (IPE)	Telengana	http://www.ipeindia.org/	1964
6	Institute of Economic Growth (IEG)	New Delhi	http://www.iegindia.org/	1958
7	Centre for the Study of Developing Societies (CSDS)	New Delhi	http://www.csds.in/	1963
8	Centre for Social Studies (CSS)	Gujarat	http://www.css.ac.in/	1969
9	Madras Institute of Development Studies (MIDS)	Tamil Nadu	http://www.mids.ac.in/	1971
10	Indian Institute of Education (IIE)	Maharashtra	http://www.iiepune.org/	1948
11	Giri Institute of Development Studies (GIDS)	Uttar Pradesh	http://www.gids.org.in/	1973
12	Centre for Policy Research (CPR)	New Delhi	http://www.cprindia.org/	1973
13	Sardar Patel Institute of Economic and Social Research (SPIESR)	Gujarat	http://www.spiesr.ac.in/	1969
14	Council for Social Development (CSD)	Andhra Pradesh	http://csdindia.org/	1967
15	Institute of Development Studies (IDS)	Rajasthan	http://www.idsj.org/	1981
16	Centre for Research in Rural and Industrial Development (CRRID)	Punjab	http://www.crrid.res.in	1978
17	Centre for Women's Development Studies (CWDS)	New Delhi	http://www.cwds.ac.in/	1980
18	Centre for Economic and Social Studies (CESS)	Andhra Pradesh	http://www.cess.ac.in	1980
19	NabakrushnaChoudhury Centre for Development Studies (NKCCDS)	Orissa	http://nkccds.nic.in/	1987
20	Gujarat Institute of Development Research (GIDR)	Gujarat	http://gidr.ac.in/	1970
21	Institute for Studies in Industrial Development (ISID)	New Delhi	www.isid.org.in	1986

Sl. No.	Name of the Institutes	States	Website URLs	Est. Year
22	O.K.D. Institute of Social Change and Development (OKDISCD)	Assam	http://www.okd.in/	1989
23	Centre for Multi-Disciplinary Development Research (CMDR)	Karnataka	http://www.cmdr.ac.in/	1976
24	Madhya Pradesh Institute of Social Science Research (MPISSR)	Madhya Pradesh	http://mpissr.org/	1983
25	Indian Institute of Dalit Studies (IIDS)	New Delhi	http://www.dalitstudies.org.in	2003
26	Asian Development Research Institute (ADRI)	Bihar	http://www.adriindia.org	1991
27	Gulati Institute of Finance and Taxation (GIFT)	Kerala	http://gift.res.in	2009
28	Institute of Development Studies Kolkata (IDSK)	West Bengal	http://idsk.edu.in	2002
29	**Institute for Human Development (IHD)**	**New Delhi**	**http://www.ihdindia.org**	1996

List of Tribal Research Institutes

S. No.	State Name	Name	Year of Establishment
1.	Andhra Pradesh	Tribal Research Institute	2014
2.	Assam	Assam Institute of Research for Tribals and Scheduled Castes	1962
3.	Andaman & Nicobar	Tribal Research Institute	2014
4.	Chhattisgarh	Tribal Research & Training Institute	2004
5.	Gujarat	Tribal Research & Training Institute	1962
6..	Himachal Pradesh	Institute of Tribals Studies	2008
7.	Jharkhand	Tribal Research Institute	1953 (undivided Bihar)
8.	Jammu & Kashmir	Tribal Research Institute	2016
9.	Kerala	Kerala Institute for Research Training & Development studies	1971
10.	Karnataka	Tribal Research Institute	2005
11.	Manipur	Tribal Research Institute	1988
12.	Madhya Pradesh	Tribal Research & Development Institute	1954
13.	Maharashtra	Tribal Research & Training Institute	1962
14.	Orissa	SC/ST Research & Training Institute	1952
15.	Rajasthan	Tribal Research & Training Institute	1964
16.	Tamil Nadu	Tribal Research Center	1983
17.	Tripura	Tribal Research & Cultural Institute	1993

S. No.	State Name	Name	Year of Establishment
18.	Uttar Pradesh	SC/ST Research & Training Institute	1972
19.	West Bengal	Cultural Research Institute	1955
20.	Sikkim	Tribal research Institute	2016
21.	Telangana	Tribal Culture Research & Training Institute	1963
22.	Uttarakhand	Tribal Research Institute	2016
23.	Nagaland	Tribal Research Institute	2018
24.	Mizoram	Tribal Research Institute	2018
25.	Arunachal Pradesh	Tribal Research Institute	2018
26.	Meghalaya	Tribal Research Institute	2018

List of Population Research Centres

The details of all the PRCs with their years of establishments and types are as follows:

Sl. No.	Name of the Centre	Name of the University/Institute where Centre is located	Year of Establishment
1	PRC, Delhi	Institute of Economic Growth, Delhi	1958
2	PRC, Kerala	University of Kerala, Trivandrum	1958
3	PRC, Dharwad	JSS Institute of Economic Research, Dharwad	1961
4	PRC, Gandhigram	Rural H&FW Trust,Gandhigram (TN)	1961
5	PRC, Pune	Gokhale Institute of Politics and Economics, Pune	1963
6	PRC, Patna	Patna University, Patna	1966
7	PRC, Lucknow	Lucknow University, Lucknow	1966
8	PRC, Baroda	MS University, Baroda	1967
9	PRC, Bangalore	Institute of Social and Economic Change, Bangalore	1972
10	PRC, Udaipur	Udaipur University, Udaipur	1977
11	PRC, Vishakhapattanam	Andhra University, Vishakhapatnam	1977
12	PRC, Guwahati	Guwahati University, Guwahati	1977
13	PRC, Bhubaneshwar	Utkal University, Bhubaneshwar	1977

Sl. No.	Name of the Centre	Name of the University/Institute where Centre is located	Year of Establishment
14	PRC, Punjab University, Chandigarh	Punjab University, Chandigarh	1978
15	PRC, Srinagar	University of Srinagar (J&K)	1985
16	PRC, CRRID Chandigarh	Centre for Research in Rural and Industrial Development (CRRID) CRRID, Chandigarh	1986
17	PRC, Shimla	Himachal University, Shimla	1988
18	PRC, Sagar	Dr. Harisingh Gour University, Sagar	1999

Industry Labs with Research Responsibility

S.No	Name	City/State	Est. Year
1	Advanced Materials and Processes Research Institute (AMPRI)	Bhopal	1981
2	Central Building Research Institute (CBRI)	Roorkee	1947
3	Centre for Cellular Molecular Biology (CCMB)	Hyderabad	1977
4	Central Drug Research Institute (CDRI)	Lucknow	1951
5	Central Electrochemical Research Institute (CECRI)	Karaikudi	1948
6	Central Electronics Engineering Research Institute (CEERI)	Pilani	1953
7	Central Food Technological Research Institute (CFTRI)	Mysore	1950
8	Central Glass Ceramic Research Institute (CGCRI)	Kolkata	1950
9	Central Institute of Medicinal Aromatic Plants (CIMAP)	Lucknow	1959
10	Central Institute of Mining and Fuel Research (CIMFR)	Dhanbad	2007
11	Central Leather Research Institute (CLRI)	Chennai	1948
12	Central Mechanical Engineering Research Institute (CMERI)	Durgapur	1958
13	Central Road Research Institute (CRRI)	New Delhi	1952
14	Central Scientific Instruments Organisation (CSIO)	Chandigarh	**1959 in New Delhi, Relocated to Chandigarh in 1962**
15	Central Salt Marine Chemicals Research Institute (CSMCRI)	Bhavnagar	1954
16	CSIR Fourth Paradigm Institute (4PI)	Bengaluru	1988
17	Institute of Genomics and Integrative Biology (IGIB)	Delhi	1977
18	Institute of Himalayan Bioresource Technology (IHBT)	Palampur	1983
19	Indian Institute of Chemical Biology (IICB)	Kolkata	1935
20	Indian Institute of Chemical Technology (IICT)	Hyderabad	1944
21	Indian Institute of Integrative Medicine (IIIM)	Jammu	1941
22	Indian Institute of Petroleum (IIP)	Dehradun	1960

S.No	Name	City/State	Est. Year
23	Indian Institute of Toxicology Research (IITR)	Lucknow	1965
24	Institute of Minerals and Materials Technology (IMMT)	Bhubaneswar	1964
25	Institute of Microbial Technology (IMTECH)	Chandigarh	1984
26	National Aerospace Laboratories (NAL)	Bengaluru	1959
27	National Botanical Research Institute (NBRI)	Lucknow	1978
28	National Chemical Laboratory (NCL)	Pune	1950
29	National Environmental Engineering Research Institute (NEERI)	Nagpur	1958
30	North – East Institute of Science and Technology (NEIST)	Jorhat	1961
31	National Geophysical Research Institute (NGRI)	Hyderabad	1961
32	National Institute For Interdisciplinary Science and Technology (NIIST)	Thiruvananthapuram	1975
33	National Institute of Oceanography (NIO)	Goa	1966
34	National Institute of Science Communication And Information Resources (NISCAIR)	New Delhi	2002
35	National Institute of Science, Technology And Development Studies (NISTADS)	New Delhi	1980
36	National Metallurgical Laboratory (NML)	Jamshedpur	1950
37	National Physical Laboratory (NPL)	New Delhi	1947
38	Structural Engineering Research Centre (SERC)	Chennai	1965
39	CSIR-UNIT: Open Source Drug Discovery (OSDD)	New Delhi	2008
40	CSIR-UNIT: Traditional Knowledge Digital Library (TKDL)	New Delhi	2001
41	CSIR-UNIT: Translational Research and Innovative Science Through Ayurveda (TRISUTRA)	New Delhi	
42	CSIR-UNIT: Human Resource Development Centre(HRDC)	Ghaziabad	
43	CSIR-UNIT: Unit for Research and Development of Information Products (URDIP)	Pune	2010
44	CSIR Madras Complex (CMC)	Chennai	1942

Despite setting an example of how research and impact studies could be conducted, these research reports have not become case examples for impact studies—neither among academics nor among TV channels, despite the proliferation of competing TV channels. SITE research was like a rainbow in that period. It vanished from the minds of even social science researchers. Today many, even in academia, do not have an idea of that experiment.

Qualitative Research Is Better

My 60 years' experience swimming through applied social research convinces me that quantitative approaches and methodologies are not enough to fully bring out the dynamics, the process of change and the undercurrents. I am also sensible of the fact that both quantitative and qualitative methods have their limits and biases. The fact that we adopted the quantitative approach from the very outset of our journey for the last 75 years explains why we have not realised our goals from the research track. In our research pursuits and preoccupations, we have not explored alternative methodologies. For example, an anthropological approach and ethnographic methodologies would have given us far more insight and sensitivity to the policy implementation problems on the ground. We have hardly explored the 'case studies' approach, for example, to explain the process of change. Our academic curriculum has been such that it did not even refer to alternative methods like the ISRO–SITE, perhaps because we adopted, so long ago, a quantitative model across the research paradigm. Our model of development, prompted by British rule and pursed over the last 75 or more years has been such that it relied more on a quantitative outlook and criteria. Short-term concerns coterminous with the cycle of elections too have preferred a quantitative orientation and perspective.

It is not that Indian ethnographic studies do not exist. The examination of caste and community by Professor M.N.

Srinivas or on caste and conflict by Professor S.C. Dube or on the dynamics of social change by Professor Damle and by Professor Dandekar on poverty in the initial years (around 1950), for example, introduced a sustainable and positive outlook towards these phenomena. Sociologist Radhakamal Mukherjee offered a good explanation for social change and social transition. Even among economists, those who adopted a qualitative approach offered better options for the future. Muhammad Yunus of Bangladesh developed better solutions to tackle poverty, inequalities and growth in his country. As did our own Amartya Sen earlier or Abhijit Banerjee more recently. Even the first batch of Development Institutes set up by economists in the state capitals were qualitative in orientation, and mostly used the case study approach. More recently Nobel awardee Abhijit Banerjee looked beyond quantitative criteria with an 'experimental method', but this has not been further explored.

Perhaps another factor hampering the diversification of research approaches is the job and employment orientation of education. The quest for quantitative growth and development swept away our concern with welfare. In that process, the interest in sustainability of development in our Five Year Plans, for example, came decades later. We also missed out on exploring 'happiness', 'harmony' and the cultural dimensions of development. We also neglect children, adolescents and older people in research coverage, as well as local specific social peculiarities.

Today the focus is less on national integration and more on homogenisation or centralisation of policies. Local or regional sentiments and differences are pushed under the carpet. Application of newer technologies ensures centralisation, at the cost of bulldozing local cultures and research models.

Politicisation of Public Policies, and Decline in Policy/Social Research

State policies are public policies. All state policies are expected to be Of, By and For the public. The idea of a policy may be politically initiated and politically motivated but once it becomes a policy in a parliamentary democracy, it cannot be partisan or considered as belonging to a particular party or leader. As a policy, it must be applicable or available to all. Prime Minister Narendra Modi gave a call to members of his ruling party on August 4, 2019, that they should serve all citizens, cutting across party lines and regardless of whom they had voted for. This piece of advice of the Prime Minister could change the face of Indian politics, and the scope of development and democracy, if only his advice is taken with earnestness by all leaders, parties and members of legislatures.

Over the years, public policies have become increasingly politically motivated and remain so even after they have been formally adopted. Members of the ruling party today call the Government the 'BJP Government' or the 'Modi Government' even inside the Parliament. Even the opposition parties in the legislatures call the Government as that of the party in power or that of the leader by name. The Government is 'India's', and 'of all people' and as such policies should be applicable to all in an inclusive way. Research and methodologies should not ignore this.

But political polarisation is evident everywhere today. The Swachh Bharat policy, for example, does not belong to the

BJP Government or Modi, as it is talked about often and viewed because of the way it is being promoted. There is a state where every policy and scheme is formally named and promoted as that of the individual leader by name or his father. Researchers tend to avoid examining this trend and its implications for the trajectory of development, democracy and governance. This trend is another factor responsible for the decline in policy and independent research.

Today many problems to do with governance in the country are because of the politicisation of policies. Because of this, the paradigm of democracy is being constrained and undermined. It is a stumbling block in our path to growth and development. As a result, leaders and parties tend to view everything, including public policies, through a partisan lens. And the research environment in the country reflects this trend. It has changed the paradigm of research, feedback, evaluation and methodologies and even the very scope of research.

Research implies an endeavour or pursuit of a larger cause, inclusive growth and efficient outcomes. There appears to be an inherent friction between the outlook of politicians today and the idea of research, particularly independent research. Acceptance of the value of research has become a factor that distinguishes certain leaders, parties and the governments. Research is a liberal concept for change and to make better sense of the world. Politics, on the other hand, is becoming increasingly conservative, limited to the pursuit of power rather than bringing about real change.

In the first twenty years after independence (1950-70) politics was characterised by consensus building and public participation, and public cooperation was sought for policies and development plans. This approach surpassed the interests of political parties. Leaders in these initial years looked towards the future and were concerned with linkages and consequences for the betterment of everyone regardless of politics. This was evident in the research paradigm and pursuits of those years. The next twenty years (1970-90) were characterised by ambitious parties and aggressive political leaders aggrandising the state. Politics was driven by the desire for influence, even domination. The next twenty years (1990-2010) were reforms-driven and saw paradigm shifts despite the proliferation of short-term political compulsions. During the years of 2010-2020, public policies came to be driven by electoral politics, the desire for control and the prioritising of image. The research preoccupation of these years reflects this trend. Research methodology too has changed from participatory to ratings to mapping, reflecting the same trend.

In the early years, it was the institutions which were at the centre of governance. Later, politicisation and vote bank politics made Indian politics individual-centric, both at the union and state levels. Despite the emergence of regional parties and leaders, individualisation in national politics has been visible and marked. People seem to prefer a strong leader. The idea of team or a cabinet form of government has lost appeal, eclipsed by the cult of personality. The tenor of research and methodologies reflects this trend.

The current style of governance, dominated by one leader, has deemphasised or discouraged independent research and given rise to 'supportive research' in the country. This trend has implications for research methodology and for research institutes. It has brought about a decline in the concern for objectivity and credibility of research and in the role of researchers. Research has come to be viewed as an ally in the partisan pursuit of power.

Despite the expansion of IITs, IIMs, universities of higher learning with research as a discipline and many Indians making a significant mark globally in academic and research in a range of subjects, there has been no spurt in research or in its application in the country. All this should have led to a much higher use of research in the country and a far more vibrant civil society.

Being a beneficiary politically of 'back room research', Prime Minister Modi apparently realised that a vacuum exists in academia. The Government established the 'PM research fellowships' for a thousand students in 2017-18. The fact that only three hundred scholars could avail of the fellowship indicates that the idea needs to be taken forward. The Indian Council of Social Science Research (ICSSR) remains sidelined, as does the University Grants Commission (UGC), in reviving research culture in the country.

In 2019, the historic Right to Information Act of 2005, which had created new hope among citizens of the country of communicating with the government and an opportunity for the government to be transparent, was diluted to the level of yet another department of the government of the day. Alongside this, research priorities and methodologies reflect the anxiety of those in power, more than the interests of governance. Since the provisions of the RTI Act are supportive of independent research, the government is making all-out efforts to scuttle the Act itself.

Research Concern in National Policies on Education

The kind of initiatives taken in the country to promote research in the first twenty years of the Republic remain unmatched to date. This research endeavour was not only in science and technology but gave equal priority to the social, economic and development sectors. That was how there came to be so many premier research institutes across the country. Most of them were set up prior to the 1970s. Private research outfits sprang up thereafter, most of them profit-oriented. With the increasing commercialisation of research, there was an influx of foreign research corporates. Research has become a commercial service in the market. Sponsor orientation and bias in research has become obvious. While research has become a competitive market, there is no evidence that the quality and objectivity of research has improved. Nor is there appreciation for independent research. Of course, the overall opportunities for research have increased in the country. However, little of it is being used, particularly by the public systems at large and for governance.

Dr K. Kasturirangan, former Chairman of ISRO, was appointed by the Government to draft the education policy in 2019. Realising that there was a vacuum in terms of research, Dr Kasturirangan's report came up with wide ranging recommendations. Kasturirangan is an eminent space scientist who has made pioneering contributions to space research. These recommendations include suggestions towards 'consolidating research as a discipline'. The report recommended setting up a National Research Foundation as a nodal agency to promote research in the country. Its core aim would be 'to seed, grow and facilitate research at academic institutions where research is currently at a nascent stage'. The report presented the conclusion that 'there is no research in most universities and colleges and lacks transparency and competitive peer reviewed research'. It also suggested creating 100 universities exclusively devoted to research by 2030. A UGC committee report of 2019 also sounded the alarm on decline in research in the country since 1990 and in the quality and relevance of research.

After more than fifty years, since the creation of the Indian Council of Social Science Research based on Dr V.K.R.V. Rao's report, a Government-appointed committee in 2019 had reminded the nation of the criticality of research in the pursuit of knowledge. Neither the first national policy on education in 1968 nor the second one in 1986 (revised in 1992) had referred to research as a discipline and the need to cultivate it in different levels and contexts.

Earlier, in 2018, a University Grants Commission (UGC) panel, headed by Professor Balaram of the Indian Institute of Science, suggested sweeping reforms to bring discipline to research at PhD and MPhil levels in the academic institutions of the country. It brought to light the practice of publishing research articles in 'predatory' journals and as presentations in conferences organised by dubious groups. This panel exposed the fake research paper racket reported earlier by the Indian Express in 2018. The panel even suggested a board for social science research with separate allocation of funds, including for a dean for research in universities to ensure quality in research and to build research capacity.

But the 2019 Union Budget, although it agreed with the idea of a National Research Foundation, did not provide any budget exclusively for it. Instead, it indicated that the Foundation should pool the research budgets of the Ministries, reallocate and coordinate their research while deciding relevance of research projects. The key areas of research indicated for the Foundation did not include any social development issues. Its focus appeared to be more on technology and on bringing research in the country under the Government's purview. Also, the 2019 Budget did not provide for universities exclusively devoted for research, as suggested by Dr Kasturirangan's report.

Has Our Academia Fallen Short?

India's educational network is one of the world's largest in terms of number of colleges, universities, professional institutes and enrolment of students. Educational institutions are both state-run and under private management. Today, India is an impressive source for managers, scientists, engineers, researchers and even entrepreneurs. Our technologists have made India proud. But if we look critically at the contribution of these higher-end academics in addressing the basic problems of the country, a blurred picture comes out. Why we are not at the top in innovation initiatives? How is it that Indian scientists in the US have earned laurels, patents and developed new technologies and application software? Despite a large network, impressive talent and highly dedicated academics, none of our institutions are in the top hundred globally (as of 2019).

Why for example, are the University of Georgia and many universities in Australia and Russia so sought after for admissions by Indians? It should have been the other way round by now.

India's own sought-after institutes have not made much difference at home. For example, in over 500 management schools, including over 25 IIMs, what kind of research on India specific concerns has there been? There are exceptions, of course, like IIM Ahmedabad or IIT Delhi. Dr Anil Gupta's research for over two decades on India's innovations at the grass roots should have triggered and scaled interest. Dr Abdul Kalam also posed this dilemma. Dr Dinesh Mohan's research at IIT Delhi, on urban transportation, made a difference as did that of Dr Jhunjhunwala of IIT Madras on the telecom sector. Only a few of these higher institutes have adopted behavioural research despite the fact that many of the basic issues confronting India are to do with attitude and behaviour causing last-mile stumbling blocks for scaling up.

There is not much social research to help diffusion of innovations. Why, for example, has India missed out on the solar revolution, having devised a solar energy policy more than a decade before China? Why did telecom technology not progress despite good strides made with the rugged telephone exchanges of C-DOT forty years ago? The courses on research methods tend to imitate foreign models. This is perhaps one reason why these research institutes did not make a big difference as was expected. ICSSR has had 4 or 5 institutes focussing on industry under its orbit for decades, like ISDS, but there is no indication of any of them making any difference to Indian industry at large. If bringing research from labs to the field or markets is important, how many of our IITs, IIMs, or our research institutes and universities can claim credit for doing so over the years?

Initiatives announced by the Prime Minister in recent years

remind us that the Government recognises the importance of research to sustain the growth momentum of the country. In its 2019 poll manifesto the ruling party had referred to R & D under the heading of 'good governance'. But at the same time there is no indication of any thrust to research culture. There is no assurance of space and scope for independent research. But, some welcome measures have been announced by the Government. First, a revival of research in academia by increasing the number of research scholarships and the amount of the scholarship. Two, the setting up of IMPRESS (Impactful Policy Research in Social Science) with special funding (2018-22) and entrusting part responsibility to ICSSR for social science research. Three, recognising more than a dozen institutes as 'eminent and excellent' including some private universities, and giving them special support. Four, endorsement of the idea of 100 universities of research in the next few years as envisioned in the National Education Policy. Next, announcement of a National Research Foundation in the 2019-20 budget (although with only a notional budgetary allocation), and last, special efforts to fill the many academic positions which have been vacant for long. But on the ground there is not only no evidence of follow up of any of the announcements, but curbs and curtailment of facilitative schemes for pursuing higher education are increasing, as if the space and scope for independent research is being consciously restricted.

Research culture in the country would receive encouragement and get revived only if the Government goes beyond rhetoric and restores sanctity of data and independence of primary sources of data. It must not dent the credibility of the data-gathering institutions by diffusing their role and standing. It needs to reconsider the ongoing practice of engaging foreign consulting agencies by the Ministries through a preferential route and at the cost of Indian talent and resources. It must restore evaluative research instead of supportive research and not snub critical faculties and initiatives. It should bring in transparency in selection and pre-approval restrictions on the pursuit of research in academic campuses. Lastly, curbs on support to higher education and centralisation of research endeavours should be abandoned.

Further, certain measures are needed to give a push to social science research in the country. These include: a) repositioning ICSSR and UGC with budgets and nodal responsibility for National Research Foundation; b) some special drive is needed to fill in a number of vacancies to do with research scholars and research faculties; c) the budget for social science research has to be specific and much higher than before; d) research methodology should be part of the syllabus at graduate level if not at higher secondary level as some schools are experimenting with. The 'art of questioning' should be part of nurturing critical faculties. As I discussed in my book, *Sustainable Good Governance, Development and Democracy* (SAGE 2019), Modi's messages could help pull India out of the traps of the past, and achieve high growth. These ideas cannot be realised fully without social science research at different levels in the country and independent research. The Ministries should realise this fact and take correctives by involving independent research or at least by not discouraging research.

Professional Associations

The Annual Science Congress in the first week of January has been held for decades since the Nehru years. It is organised on different academic campuses across the country. In January 2017 the Indian Science Congress, scheduled at Osmania University, Hyderabad, was cancelled for the first time because of alleged student unrest there. There were others who alleged that it was cancelled as an anti-Modi campaign was at its height there at the time. The Science Congress is always inaugurated by the Prime Minister of the country with a keynote address affirming the Government's support for scientific research. It has become a forum for exchange of new research and perspectives. This event is an annual endorsement of the Government's policy and support for scientific pursuits in the country. The Indian Science Academy has kept its stature as an independent body. It has ensured that different viewpoints are allowed at its conferences. Most papers presented and discussed in this meet are research based. Every year there are papers presented which are based on Indian ethos and original methodologies. The other professional academic bodies from the disciplines of History, Sociology, Economics, Psychology, Political Science, etc. used to have similar annual meets to introspect. Of late, however, government support to such meets seems to have dried up.

The Indian Council of Social Science Research (ICSSR) was expected to make a difference in the extent, quality and status of social research in the country. It is now more than 60 years old. Never has the PM or any other high government office holder presided over any meet of ICSSR. While it has organised and sponsored a series of short term programmes on research methodologies over these years, ICSSR never took initiatives similar to the Science Congress to bring together social science researchers or academia.

A review of ICSSR activities, priorities and focus indicates the path and likely progress of social research in the country. First, the budget of ICSSR over the years has remained low or marginal and on the decline. The scope of the educational system has increased several fold during the last 60 years, but ICSSR's activities have neither expanded nor intensified nor undergone any strategic changes. As a result, ICSSR today is not of much consequence. It has made little difference to any aspect of social research or its utilisation. It has done little to develop research methodologies to study the peculiarities of India.

There are several areas where ICSSR should have taken an interest by way of sponsoring or promoting studies. One is the social impact of television, as its proliferation and viewership has gone up significantly, changing the attitudes and life styles of people across socioeconomic divides. Two–thirds of viewership is children and women. No other intervention has changed the extent of violence against women as TV programmes. This was not an overnight phenomenon, but has unfolded over the last 25 years. It is a trend that has not been studied by any academics from a social impact perspective. Professor G.N.S. Raghavan and I tried to do so in our book *Social Effects of Mass Media in India* (1996). Even more glaringly, as TRP research by TAM (Television Audience Measurement) swayed policies, the perceptions of people, and the model of broadcasting, there has been no study as to what the TRP was all about and what this model of broadcasting meant to India, particularly because this TRP methodology has eclipsed other research initiatives in the country.

Similarly, on the multiple initiatives taken to strengthen rural communities, there has been no independent research on the future of villages of India, or the transition of 'little republics' to 'colonies of Government' and people becoming more and more dependent on government doles and 'welfare'. ICSSR is well placed to conduct such research.

ICSSR should have been concerned about the research priorities and methodologies being used in the country. There have been many books and studies on research methodologies by foreigners and all of them have, by and large, echoed and reinforced the same study methodologies.

The concern of social research has shifted over the past 60 or so years. Earlier, it was monitoring, assessing the impact and implications of policies, programmes and schemes. With foreign players (consultants and researchers) becoming active, the research methodology shifted to agenda setting and centralisation. By 2010, this had shifted again to rating and ranking where the comparative context is globalisation and commercial interests. Now, by 2020-2023, the thrust, directly and indirectly, is towards supportive and endorsement research.

6

IS 'INDEPENDENT' RESEARCH ON THE WAY OUT?

Independent Research Outfits

No research is an end in itself. This is particularly true of research to do with public policies and issues relating to society, politics, economies and governance. Different sections of the public avail of research for different purposes. Those in government tend to use it to strengthen their own grip, those in advertising and marketing use research to persuade and promote, many others use research to change behaviours and perceptions. Many also avail of research to explore options, find correctives, understand outcomes and for perspectives on the future. Who conducts research, what is the source of data, what is the scope and structure of the organisation responsible—these determine the credibility of the research. Whether the public is concerned about these aspects is doubtful. But it is important that these aspects should be in the public knowledge.

With research becoming a business proposition, and even big corporates taking to research, the credibility of the findings often come under increasing questioning. Particularly when those findings are used to influence, or make a profit by controlling data and manipulating research. The reliability, objectivity and transparency of research helps minimise such threats to the efficacy of the research itself. Validation, and provisions for checks and verification determines the credibility of research findings. For research conducted for public policy on socio-economic issues, credibility matters even more. When research is conducted by 'independent' agencies, credibility is expected or presumed to be better than otherwise. When a public trust or foundation conducts research or sponsors research on specific issues, the outcome is presumed to be trustworthy. This is because of the legal provisions of such organisations which, apart from being non-profit, are expected to follow certain self-imposed obligations and make the process and outcome of such research transparent and responsible.

Any research organisation, irrespective of its legal stature, can do a particular piece of research objectively, independently, avoiding influence or bias or any conflict of interest. The bias can come in at any stage of research from conceptualising, designing the study, selection of methodology, designing instruments used to collect primary data, and in analysing and in writing the report itself and even the timing of the research. An independent organisation is expected to be transparent about such practices and about its overall operations in conducting the research.

Criteria to Be Considered Independent

An independent research outfit should stand out as distinct in its practices and positioning. Some of the elements of independence, apart from its formal organisational nature, include the following.

First, an independent research body, to uphold itself, must have concerns of its own which it believes in as a pursuit. Governance, children and women or civic society or citizen activism, for example, could be the concerns of a research organisation.

Second, it should operate as an institution which is an ongoing or continuing body with long-term interests, and does not operate on a project-to-project basis. It should not be individual-centric even if it has been set up or guided by one particular person.

Third, it must have a wide ranging data base, such as reports of the Census, NFHS, ASER, etc. This includes having a library with access to extensive reference sources—books, reports, or software and digital data bases.

Fourth, it should have a team of experts specialising in a range of subjects like demography, economy, geography, etc. They should be able to design research, conduct field work, analyse and write reports.

Fifth, it must have infrastructure, including a reference library, analytical tools, application packages, consultation back up, and a field network to conduct field studies.

Sixth, it must have standard validation procedures. For example, having an Ethical Committee, to assess whether a particular piece of research is following the standard procedures, whether anyone is likely to be disadvantaged or harmed by it, whether such a study undermines prevailing regulations, etc.

Seventh, it conducts studies which enhance its capabilities, and constantly improves its own procedures and practices. For example, it should conduct a validation of its methodologies before adopting them. Learning should be evident in that process.

Eighth, it shares its research and findings in different ways so that many others benefit from the research findings.

Ninth, it must be transparent in its functioning, complying with regulations of the profession, government and regulatory provisions

Tenth, it never hesitates to offer insights for policy formulation and correction, shares suggestions in crisis situations as a part of public service.

Eleventh, it remains a not-for-profit body and sustains its viability in such a way that it does not have to succumb to market forces or sponsor's interests, and can avoid external support from doubtful backgrounds.

Twelfth, as an independent institute, it should follow as many of these self-prescribed principles as norms or protocols in such a way that its independence is never questioned.

There are several Indian-origin institutes who have enriched the national discourse and sustained themselves without compromising their core concerns and independence. Of over a hundred legitimate research organisations engaged in India in applied or operational or behavioural research, there are perhaps around a dozen truly independent ones. Many of these are independent of any affiliations, political or corporate origins. They are distinguished for one or other specialisation or attribute despite being multifaceted. Of those which have lasted three decades and more, CSDS, CSD, CMS, CSE and CPR stand out in terms of research quality and transparency. There are of course many others. As independent research organisations in the public domain, these have distinguished themselves from others including many state-funded institutes described as 'autonomous'. I have had first-hand acquaintanceship with most of them over the years, and even more closely with ORG and CMS for much longer. These independent organisations have contributed original activities and initiatives, and distinguished themselves over those pursuing sponsored research.

I have witnessed, during my active years at ORG (1972-89) and at CMS thereafter (1989-2023), what this 'third eye position' of research is all about. A third eye view could also be taken by research agencies without being independent. But only a few organisations maintained such a position beyond a couple of decades.

How Independent, Over the Years

To be truly independent, a research organisation has to demonstrate that independent character in all its operations. I would like to suggest six core characteristics here. It should not depend for its viability on any external support of any kind, knowingly or unknowingly. Its source of revenue should not be from any outside source beyond the scope of research. It should sustain itself from resources generated from within, as far as possible. It should not pursue profit or have any conflict of interest. It should not seek or derive favours from clients or the government. It should be sensitive to the quid-pro-quo possibility that research often gets lured into. None of this is possible unless an organisation is run with a certain discipline, commitment and with low establishment expenses and self-motivated professionals on its team.

Most research agencies go through a viability dilemma. While independent research plays the role of the third eye of governance, how do research agencies sustain themselves? CSDS, CSE, and CMS undertake multiple activities simultaneously, but all originating from research. CMS, for example, demonstrated its third eye function by taking several initiatives in the larger public interest. Among these were a first-of-its-kind 'media lab' to track the agenda-setting process. It conducts periodic field surveys on larger public concerns like corruption in basic public services. It audits the performance of Ministries as well as the judiciary, and conducts impact studies on flagship public schemes. It also conducted the first social audit in India, and organises the country-wide Vatavaran programme which is now a twenty-year-long running movement. All these initiatives have positioned CMS as an independent research based think-tank with a credible advocacy role.

Professional research services belong to different streams. Three types are indicated here, with a few examples. Also, three different 'independent research service' (ADR, ASER, NFHS) are specially mentioned here as examples of what a consortium of agencies could offer as an 'independent service'. The organisations I refer to here as examples from different categories of service are the ones I am more familiar with. I have devoted more space to CMS as I know about it first-hand.

Market Research, the Origin of Applied Research

Market research including advertising and consumer research was the launchpad for policy, social research and survey research in the country. Despite several-fold growth in policy/social research, the reliance on market research continues today. The dominant influence of market research is evident on policy research. Even academics have been using broadly the same research methodologies. The credit for this in India goes to the Operations Research Group (formed in 1961) which is known popularly as ORG. Despite originating from the Sarabhai industry house, it has spear-headed survey research in India, and monitoring and evaluative research on a syndicate basis. In fact, it was the launchpad for research for wide-ranging studies in the industry, government and civil society (from 1970 to 1990).

Many research organisations today are rooted in ORG. A number of local smaller research groups sprang up after 1972. A few big multinational market research outfits too started. MARG (Marketing Research Group), MODE, MRAS, IMRB, which entered as a division of British Marketing Research Group, became active. Most market research companies came out of ORG or later from IMRB. Similarly, after 2000 many researchers came from CMS.

Initially, industry and marketing companies availed of research far more than the government even though the government's task to reach out and create awareness and motivation is much bigger. Most market research firms in India today are controlled by or are part of a multinational corporate. They also dominate advertising and corporate research, and many are also engaged in PR and lobbying. Truly Indian ones have less than 20 per cent market share of research outlays.

ORG: Operations Research Group (1965-95), as India's foremost market research organisation, was the fountainhead of marketing and consumer research. It also pioneered social and pharma research in India. For almost a decade (1967-77), ORG was the sole research outfit of the country outside the government. IMRB (Indian Market Research Bureau) started its operations in India in 1972, followed by MARG (1976), MRAS or Market Research as a Service (1978) and a couple of other splinter groups. ORG was also the first research organisation to have dedicated field researchers covering most parts of India including rural areas. But by 1975 there were other agencies carrying out consumer and market research, mostly identified with particular individuals like Titoo Ahluwalia. By 1995 there was a huge influx of foreign research agencies in India. In the process, Indian research agencies like ORG disappeared. Today, of about 25 market research, data and consulting groups, hardly 6 or 7 are Indian in origin. The government itself started preferring foreign research agencies even when it was known that they had neither the track record nor data base and despite the fact that they were much more expensive.

Most market research organisations today are affiliated to a business group or foreign multinational affiliated to global corporates. Even their activities have slowed down. E-surveys and video calls are being relied on more to touch base with the grassroots. There are very few Indian market research firms now left in the country.

ORG was the first to introduce the idea of syndicated research. It was also the first organisation to have country-wide full-time field investigating teams trained to collect basic data and conduct person-to-person interviews, even on sensitive topics. Among its flagship schemes were retail store audits of consumer products, pharma audits of drug stores, prescription audits and press advertising audits, some of which were used by foreign firms. Large-scale country-wide sample surveys were pioneered by ORG. It had a data base which many government departments relied upon.

This state-of-the-art organisation was made to disappear in a matter of a couple of years. In fact, the other key research organisations like MODE and MARG were also engulfed in no time after 1995. All these Indian research agencies were merged into AC Neilson or Kantar, which did not even acknowledge the data bases of Indian agencies. The era of Indian market research, which lasted thirty-five years (1965-2000), ended by 2000. Not only did a Western model of research take root, but a new phase of quantitative research changed the very structure and scope of research in India. Now the digital era is taking root. An Indian model of research ceased to exist even in academic institutions including the IIMs, with no one seemingly even aware of the transition. Television research by way of TRP has dominated and dictated the contents of channels and gripped the households and even derailed Indian TV into a copycat industry. And yet no time series research was ever contemplated.

ORG was acquired by AC Nielsen in 1990 and merged its services and data bases. Initially ORG's name was acknowledged but after a couple of years the ORG name was removed, despite the fact that those services were initiated and given credibility by ORG. ORG was India's first truly independent research body, not just in market and consumer research but also in social research. In both fields it was the pioneer of field and survey research.

MARG (1976-2000): The story of MARG's exit was similar to ORG's, once it made its reputation. AC Nielsen acquired it and removed the name of MARG. Unlike in the case of ORG, MARG eroded itself from within as it was unable to direct its field staff.

MDRA (formed in 1990): Marketing Development Research Associates is a private limited concern. The 30-year-old organisation is engaged in a wide range of research studies. Its credibility is demonstrated by the fact that competing market players, including prominent media establishments, rely on its services. So do industry organisations like CII. Its methodologies in tracking educational institutes and public utilities are well known and even used by the World Bank and other such international outfits. Although it is a private limited company, it operates as an independent research agency. It is not part of any industry nor does it have any lobbying interests. It is a truly professional research group. Its *State of states of India 2022-23* is a reminder of its extensive and objective research database. It has set an example for the role research bodies could play in synthesizing data and analytics. Aroon Purie, Editor-in-chief of *India Today*, its parent body, which has been ranking the states of India on performance criteria for over two decades, described MDRA in an editorial as 'credible, authenticated data' for rankings.

Many private research firms are offspring or associates of market research companies. Although there are many of them, more than 80 per cent of research turnover is handled by just six or seven consulting or research organisations and all of them are foreign based, with only a few of them registered in India. Only a couple of the Indian private limited ones are three decades old or more. Most of them are one-person centric. Hardly any have acquired institutional character or functioning. Only a couple of such private limited companies which are of Indian origin and have existed for over 25 years are referred to here. These include CMIE (Centre for Monitoring Indian Economy), MDRA, DRS (Development and Research Services) and Hansa Research.

Chennai-based Hansa is an associate of R.K. Swamy Advertising Associates. However, it has engaged in important research projects. In terms of volume of business, DRS (Development & Research Services) stands out. It is engaged in doing mostly Government research assignments of large volume. Fairly active, DRS is established and stable. It was founded by a senior researcher coming out of CMS. It is run now actively by his family members as its founder is active in party politics.

Not 'Not-for-profit', But Independent

Even without being legally 'non-profit' in character, a research agency can function independently. If such an organisation has been in existence for three decades or more without any conflict of interest, it could be considered as independent. Particularly when it is multi-faceted and catering to clientele in the corporate, government and media sectors simultaneously. Do we have any such organisation which originated within India and remained independent without becoming a partner of a foreign agency or coming under their control even on a project to project basis? Only a couple of such organisations can be named.

CMIE (1976): The Centre for Monitoring Indian Economy is an independent private limited entity that serves both as an economic think-tank as well as a business information company. CMIE research group has built credible databases on the Indian economy and private companies. It provides much relied-upon databases and research reports periodically. They are available as a syndicated service. It has one of the longest-standing independent credible data bases, often causing concern to the Government by differing with its claims, but sustaining itself based on its reliability and promptness. CMIE was the brain child of some of the finest Indian economists, among them Professor D. T. Lakdawala, a respected economist of the 1960s.

'Autonomous', But Not Independent!

There are outfits set up by one or other Ministry of the Government. Although autonomous on paper, they are controlled and directed by the concerned Ministry in every respect. Six examples are given here—NIHFW (National Institute of Health and Family Welfare), NIRDPR (National Institute of Rural Development and Panchayati Raj), IICA (Indian Institute of Corporate Affairs), NILEM (National Institute of Labour Education and Management), CESS (Centre for Economic and Social Studies) and NCAER (National Council of Applied Economic Research) These were set up for research, training, data bases and consultancy by various Ministries. They never acquired a research base, strength and status. Today they are mostly engaged in organising workshops at the instance of the Ministry. Any occasional research conducted is in support of the Ministry's interests. None of these autonomous institutes have acquired an independent status though they are mostly registered under the Societies Act as non-profit.

'Autonomous' is how many of these government-directed institutes describe themselves. Although they are structured as 'societies', they operate as extensions of the concerned Ministry. They have neither the advantage of being a Government department nor of an independent institute. Hardly any of these organisations like NIPCED, NIRD, IIFD, NILEM, NIHFW have done any research of significance in recent years, although that is still their mandate. They have largely been confined to training and monitoring. In earlier years, some of them, like the National Institute of Nutrition did some landmark studies, as did the Indian Institute of Labour. These few examples only remind us how far they have drifted.

NCAER (1959) is India's oldest and largest non-profit, economic policy research think- tank. It has acquired considerable national and international standing for its professional and independent functioning, despite being supported by the Government. It is one of a handful of think-tanks globally that combine rigorous analysis and data collection capabilities, especially for household surveys. With international standing for its analysis and data collection from field surveys with a multidisciplinary approach (encompassing growth, investment, poverty, human development, consumer behaviour), its empirical evidence is widely acknowledged. In 2017, it set up NCAER National Data Innovation Centre to experiment with data collection and analysis. But it has been somewhat dormant of late. It deserves its pioneering status back.

NIRD: (National Institute of Rural Development, 1960) Its mission includes training community development functionaries and undertaking research studies. On being shifted from Mussoorie to a huge campus in Rajindra Nagar on the outskirts of Hyderabad several years ago, it took up research studies in an isolated way on the functioning of grassroots agencies. But with Panchayati Raj added to its task, it has become more a training institute for Panchayati Raj institutions and monitoring. It is not known for any particular research or even monitoring on any aspects to do with rural development and decentralisation.

NIHFW: (The National Institute of Health and Family Welfare, 1977) This is an autonomous organization under the Ministry of Health and Family Welfare. It is expected to be an 'apex technical institute' as well as a 'think tank' for the promotion of health and family welfare programmes. It has an impressive campus in the heart of south Delhi. Over the last decade no research has come out of it, nor has any 'technical' support to the Ministry been heard about. The institute is languishing with many vacancies, particularly in the research department. Since I was on its executive board for two terms during its heyday, I know its potential. It did not even follow up the vast data of the National Family Health Surveys over the last decade with any analysis, which is left to foreign agencies like PEW. NIHFW is confined mostly to training, and its research agenda seems to have been abandoned.

CESS: (The Centre for Economic and Social Studies, 1980) is an autonomous research institute of the Andhra Pradesh Government to facilitate research in economics and social sciences. B.P.R. Vithal, a former Principal Secretary to the Government of Andhra Pradesh, took the initiative to set up this institute in Hyderabad. Initially, it contributed with its research studies on poverty, rural development, agriculture and food security. More recently in the last decade no research of any significance has come out of CESS as the state government engages foreign consulting firms. CESS is occupied now with occasional conferences.

NILEM: NILEM (National Institute of Labour Education and Management, 2009) is an educational organization run on 'no loss and no profit' basis. Initially NILEM launched short-term educational courses and conducted research and evaluation studies. For the last few years nothing has been heard of their research initiatives due to crunch of funds, cut in budget and ambivalence in public policies of the Government on labour issues. It outsources research assignments to outside research outfits.

Indian Institute of Corporate Affairs: (IICA, 2008) is a research and training institute of the Ministry of Corporate Affairs. It runs flagship programmes on Insolvency and CSR on behalf of the Ministry. It is expected to conduct Impact Assessment, Need Assessment, Baseline surveys, Real time monitoring, etc. but there is no record of any of those being carried out. I was on the board for two years, and interacted with its senior staff. A huge campus in Gurgaon was inaugurated by the PM several years ago. The building was so huge that hardly one-fourth is ever utilised. It claims to include Schools of Corporate Law, Competition Law and Market Regulations, Corporate Governance and Public Policy and Finance. And also, on paper, Centres for Business Innovation, Insolvency and Bankruptcy, Environment and Sustainable Development. It is not known for any research or analysis and instead endorses the Ministry's claims.

Foreign Research Outfits

There are active research outfits in India like AC Neilson, IMRB and Kantor who have been operating for over three decades, but they are fully foreign conglomerates. Agencies like KPMG, McKinsey, Deloitte and Ernst & Young, which are extensively relied on by the government, are all global corporates originating from the USA or UK.

The research involved in 'consultancy assignments' is mostly carried out by foreign research and consultancy organisations, who in turn 'outsource' to local individuals. As a result of this, serious research has not received special focus. The origins and affiliation of many of these foreign agencies is well-known. To be described as 'independent research institutes' they should have continuity, and their own infrastructure including field staff and data bases. Foreign consulting agencies should support local initiatives and strengthen local identities.

The government tends to prefer multinational research agencies while assigning research projects even on contentious topics. This takes place even when not much is known about those research agencies as to their origin, affiliation, ownership and control and even when the research project in question requires local understanding and respect for local culture and sensitivities. For the last couple of decades, it has been made easy for foreign research and marketing and advertising and consultancy agencies to operate in India and generate data of all kinds, including on vital socio-economic parameters. In some cases the research agency is an associate or affiliate of a market research or advertising or a public relations firm whose origin and affiliations also are not known or clear. An example is how the TRP system of rating TV channels and their programmes was brought in, which swiftly took over the Indian scene. The agency which conducted and offered TRP services was not known in the initial years. For over 15 years TRPs have shaped the lifestyles of Indians, unhindered.

Using the RTI Act, *The Indian Express*, revealed in November 2023 that 16 union ministries and 50 departments had outsourced several critical research assignments to multinational consultancy firms. Between 2017 and 2022, the Big Four—PricewaterhouseCoopers (PwC), Deloitte Touche Tohmatsu Limited, Ernst & Young Global Limited, KPMG International Limited—and the US-based McKinsey & Company were assigned more than 300 assignments worth Rs 500 to 750 crore from various government ministries, departments and organisations, including the Niti Aayog. The Government roped in these foreign consultant agencies as if it were 'on the brink of relinquishing its hold', according to the Ken report of June 2023.

Independent Research Reports

ADR, ASER and NHFS reports are a good example of how independent research could offer new insights. These are based on original field data collected using specially devised methodologies. These three research services use a consortium approach where collaborators include private companies, society and education institutions sponsored by the government. ADR includes state-wide players, of which many are non-profit, and collaborates with the Election Commission of India. ADR's primary reports are based on the filings by contesting candidates every time there is an election for Parliament or Assembly under the Election Commission of India. ASER, started by non-profit independent Pratham, collaborates with local agencies in states for field work in schools. The NHFS, although coordinated by a Government-sponsored Institute, includes a number of state-wise research agencies, and not all of them are non-profit.

ADR: The Association for Democratic Reforms came into existence in 1999 when a group of Professors from the Indian Institute of Management (IIM) Ahmedabad and Bangalore filed a Public Interest Litigation (PIL) with the Delhi High Court regarding the disclosure of the criminal, financial and educational background of the candidates contesting elections to legislatures. The PIL was upheld by the Delhi High Court in 2000, but the Government of India appealed to the Supreme Court of India against the High Court judgement. However, in 2003, the Supreme Court made it mandatory for all the candidates contesting elections to disclose their criminal, financial and educational background prior to the polls by filing an affidavit with the Election Commission of India. ADR analyses the nominations, which the Election Commission shares, and brings out reports in the context of every election and in such a way that the analysis is in the public domain. The process has led to greater awareness among voters about criminal cases against politicians. The objective of ADR is to improve governance and strengthen democracy by continuous analyses and research in the area of Electoral and Political Reforms. The impact of these impressive initiatives of ADR is yet to be independently studied, but their efforts over the years are much needed and appreciated.

ASER (2008): ASER Centre is a specialized, independent unit within the Pratham network, in order to institutionalize and strengthen the design and process of school outcomes at various levels. As one of the prominent non-governmental organizations in the country, Pratham focuses on high-quality, low-cost and replicable interventions to address gaps in the education system. It has demonstrated impact on children's learning outcomes and its methodology is now being adapted to contexts outside India. ASER reports are aimed at improving educational outcomes in the country. Are social sector programs aimed at the school-going leading to the desired outcomes? In other words, is public expenditure effectively leading towards the stated education goals? ASER has been generating results which are locally useful and allow aggregation at district and state levels to facilitate local initiatives. While internal evaluation and self-regulation by the government are clearly important for program implementation, independent assessment is critical to ensure transparency and accountability. ASER reports have now acquired much needed reliability and relevance for interventions not only by the Government, but also by schools themselves.

The National Family Health Survey (NFHS): is a large-scale, national multi-round survey conducted in a representative sample of households. The NFHS started initially as a collaborative project of the International Institute for Population Sciences (IIPS), Mumbai, and the East-West Center, Honolulu, USA. The Ministry of Health and Family Welfare designated IIPS as the nodal agency, responsible for providing coordination and technical guidance for the NFHS. NFHS was an initiative of the USAID with supplementary support from United Nations International Children's Emergency Fund (UNICEF). IIPS collaborated with a number of Field Organizations for survey implementation. Each field organisation is responsible for conducting survey activities in one or more states covered by the NFHS. Its reports are used for program planning and evaluation by the Government. Till 2023, five rounds of reports had been brought out, each with a wealth of data and insights, state wise and nationally.

Not for Profit, and Independent

CSDS (1963): The Centre for the Study of Developing Societies (CSDS) is a long-standing and widely-known independent Indian research outfit for the social sciences. It pioneered survey research on a wide range of national issues, focussing on electoral practices and representative politics. It has established itself as a credible institution with professionals from a range of disciplines. Because of its reliable research credentials, it attracts support from foreign funding agencies as much as from Indian clientele including news media. It stands out as a good example as an independent research outfit of substance. CSDS collaborated with ICSSR in earlier years in conducting courses on research methodology.

CSD: The Council for Social Development (1970) is an independent non-profit research outfit. Founded by activist–doyen of social welfare Dr Durgabhai Deshmukh, it conducted studies, based on which it advocated for special policies for children and women in the earlier years. CSD has made its mark as a leading social science research institution with a focus on education, health and nutrition, poverty, rural development, gender and social discrimination especially with reference to the marginalised communities. All this was in the earlier decades. Despite having its own campus prominently located in New Delhi, it has been languishing in last decade for lack of direction, support and professionals.

CPR (1973): The Centre for Policy Research is a think-tank, and a not-for-profit outfit. It receives grants from a variety of domestic and international sources, including governments and multilateral agencies. Initially it relied on Government funding. It describes itself as a 'non-partisan independent institution dedicated to conducting research that contributes to high quality scholarship, better policies, and a more robust public discourse about the issues that impact life in India'. Over the decades CPR has made significant contributions as a third eye. Its strengths include independent research by a number of scholars and experienced bureaucrats. CPR is known for sharing its research and analysis in the public interest. When in March 2023 its FCRA (Foreign Contribution Regulation Act) clearance was withdrawn, depriving it of foreign funding on alleged violation of provisions, the *Hindu* editorialised (on March 6, 2023) the suspension of CPR's FCRA as 'an attack on knowledge' and 'hostility towards knowledge creation of all kinds'. It also stated that 'the Government should not merely tolerate, but facilitate the emergence of several more institutions such as the CPR'.

CSE: Centre for Science and Environment (1980) is a not-for-profit public interest research and advocacy organisation. CSE works as a think tank on environment and development issues in India, and brings sensitivities on climate shifts and advocates for policy changes and better implementation of the already existing policies. CSE had exposed, based on research, the presence of high levels of pesticides in soft drinks like Coke and Pepsi. In 2018, the CSE was awarded the Indira Gandhi Prize for Peace, Disarmament and Development. Some of its projects include investigating food adulteration and consumer product safety. Its longstanding flagship magazine, *Down to Earth* (English & Hindi) has been very actively sensitising different sections of society, including the younger age groups. CSE has inducted many young academics into the field of environment research.

PAC: Public Affairs Centre (1994) is a Bangalore-based not-for-profit research think-tank. Eminent economics teacher and management professional Samuel Paul founded PAC on his retirement from IIM, Ahmedabad. It is one of the few independent research outfits which took off in the last two decades. It conducts research studies in two major fields, public policy and participatory governance. Based on its research, it publishes Citizen Report Cards to improve public services. This card has generated objective and credible citizen feedback on issues to do with delivery of public services. Ford Foundation and National Foundation for India financially supported it initially. Now the State Government of Karnataka is a major supporter. Until recently, PAC measured the quality of governance of Indian states. Using the UN SDG indicators, it brings out an annual index, whose themes are equity, growth and sustainability. It assesses accountability, Government effectiveness, rule of law and regulatory quality. Its Public Affairs Index of states of India, since 2011, is objective and inclusive.

GRAAM: (Grassroots Research and Advocacy Movement) is a Mysore-based research, skill-imparting independent outfit. Its focus is on action research and policy formulation and consultation at the grassroots. It is one of few to reflect grassroots voices. It also offers workshops on research methodologies on its own and sponsored by ICSSR.

PHFI (2006): Public Health Foundation of India has been a research based policy and training institute in four locations of the country. In no time it earned credibility for its research on health policies, programmes and perspectives under the direction of eminent cardiologist Dr K. Srinath Reddy. Although initially sponsored by the Ministry of Health, it remained an autonomously governed public private initiative. As it started an anti-smoking campaign based on its 2017 research on tobacco consumption, going against the interests of the tobacco industry, it lost sponsorship. The government subsequently ignored this truly Indian initiative and prestigious national outfit.

CMS: Sustaining Itself from Within

'CMS was ten years ahead when I was in post-graduation. It continues to be considered as repository of reference by me in the class and guided many of us. It provided basic data and analysis to think beyond.' This was what Prof. Ruchi Jaggi, Director of Symbiosis Institute of Media and Communication said in a conference on curriculum development in 2021.

Founded in 1990, CMS must have given an opportunity to over 1000 youngsters in survey research and inducted as many into research studies. It has conducted one or more studies in every district of the country using a combination of research methodologies.

CMS research concerns cut across the trajectory of development, democracy and governance. This includes the pillars of the State including the media and all features involving checks and balances. Its research has been more for motivation and persuasion than for the control and command interests of political regimes. It performed the 'third eye' role for many public schemes by tracking and pointing to correctives. Many of its research findings too suffered the 'rainbow' effect of being transitory. But then they are not expected to last long, given the dynamic nature of news media in the country, particularly given the glut of political controversies that the country is preoccupied with. Research findings are forgotten too soon, even when the research has turning point or milestone significance.

CMS is not limited to two or three topics in its concerns and activities. Rather it covers wide-ranging topics of consequence to the larger public. It constantly endeavours to develop research methodologies and correct the ones in use. And it ensures that the research and analysis tools used are free from bias. CMS is one of only a couple of research agencies in the country which has regular full-time trained field researchers and supervisors for validation of primary data collected. CMS has built essential infrastructure and establishment for doing professional and dispassionate field research and generate reliable primary data. CMS has been able to sustain itself for over thirty years because of its self-motivated full-time team of researchers and panel of experts on different themes.

CMS worked with justice P.B. Sawant, Chair of the Press Council (1988-92) in formulating drafts of the Right to Information legislation, based on the field experiences of Aruna Roy in Rajasthan and others in Karnataka and MP. In a proactive initiative it was CMS which, on appointment of Information Commissioners by States, invited them to an induction meet at Hyderabad Staff College of India and it was this two-day meet that helped Information Commissions in India come into play promptly within weeks after their formation in 2005-06. This initiative was followed up with the launch of a bimonthly journal, *Transparency Review*, to report on the implementation of the Act around the country and create local voluntary networks of active citizens. The journal continues since 2006.

CMS follows rigorous scrutiny and consultations before taking up its research. It is the only research agency which has an Ethical Review Board which includes outside professionals. Equally important, it collaborates with other not-for-profit field organisations so that research acquires a larger reach, spreads sensitivities and evokes concern in citizens. For example, local civil society organisations were involved in the Vatavaran films, the school library project of BREAD, or the *Library of Biographies in Mudunuru* village.

CMS never sought government grants at any level. Nor has it availed of grants or contribution from any source, at home or abroad, individuals or corporates. It conducts research projects obtained through competitive bids and on merit of its study methodology and subject specialisation. One fourth of its research activities were self-initiated.

The Social Audit idea featured the practice of 'public hearings' with stakeholders, with which two former Chief Justices of India (Justice P.N. Bhagwati and Justice R.S. Pathak) were associated. The Citizen Charter was reviewed across 65 Union departments and suggested periodic changes in the charters.

As a part of its pursuit on Good Governance, CMS developed methodology to focus on exposing corruption that citizens experience in availing of the 18 most used public services including the judiciary. Through its 'Vatavaran' idea, CMS took 'mission environment' across the country, even more vigorously in the Himalayan foothills, and 'river city clusters' focussing on younger age groups. It organised CMS Vatavaran festivals in some 43 cities spread across the country. These studies were taken up by CMS on its own with its own research and resources. CMS believes that research is not an end in itself but a means to make governance public-centric and responsible for upholding the 'We the People' idea. No wonder that a Cabinet Secretory (B. G. Deshmukh) on his retirement visited CMS first to acquaint himself with the concerns of vulnerable people. Another Cabinet Secretary invited the DG of CMS to be on the Cabinet Review Committee on targets and outcome of Union Ministries.

The series of public lectures it organises are highly

appreciated for their relevance. The most remembered include its 15 lectures on 'Challenges and Opportunities of the New Millennium' in 2002 and 16 lectures on 'Analysing and Envisioning India' in 2010-2011.

These national lectures were given by eminent personalities who have made a difference in the country. These include Dr V. Kurien, Dr Ela Bhatt, Dr M.S. Swaminathan, Dr Ashish Bose, Dr R.A. Mashelkar, Nandan Nilekani, Dr Srinath Reddy, B.G. Verghese, Dr L.M. Singhvi, N. Vittal and Dr Kasturi Rangan, among others.

Over the years CMS prepared guidelines for the 'Best Practices' on critical or contentious issues. Its public service programmes spread across 12 to 14 cities of the country. The themes range from children to impact of TV news, to upholding RTI. It organises meets on several public policy formulations or review of their implementation.

In more recent years CMS has slowed down its public service activities including interactive public programmes, third eye research activities like the annual survey on corruption and 'note for vote' studies during elections at various levels which it was doing as a public service for over two decades.

What Does All this Mean?

Most of these independent research institutes, like CSE, CSDS, CPR and CMS, have slowed down in the last couple of years of their research operations. Some pioneers like ORG ceased much earlier. I know first-hand that many of these independent research institutes find it hard to maintain the kind of rigor and reliability that research requires. An apprehension, that independent research may not be favourable to the powers in the government, could be one reason for the decline in their engagement. A rise in 'supportive research' obviously implies a certain decline in independent research. This is more to do with government prescriptions, procedures and priorities, not because of economic inflation or the post-Covid situation. That trend has been gradual in more recent years as a result of control and command regimes consolidating centralisation, political control and electoral grip.

Research assignments are no longer available, with a steep decline in Governments commissioning research and evaluation. None of the Ministries/Departments concerned with complex subjects and involving a wide section of people have sought research or data from independent sources. The last one was in 2018-19, to do with Swachh Bharat. If and when any research is required, it is assigned to a foreign corporate research agency, as if it was more for PR, or to a unknown research outfit or one which is more likely to give a 'suitable' report. The net result is that the ones with experience and much-needed data bases for analyses and perspective are not preferred. The impression is that the Government thinks that allowing foreign research outfits into India without any special accountability and even giving them preferential opportunities will enhance the global standing of the country. These foreign research and consulting agencies are given preferential treatment in terms of access to data and government offices. But there is no evidence of any advantage for the country even in the more recent decades. In fact, it is these very foreign research agencies which support those foreign powers, including those involved in formulating and promoting key Global Indexes.

Overall, the research culture and climate itself is experiencing a setback and some agencies have been derailed altogether. Some Institutes under one or other Ministry are also languishing because there are no researchers on the staff or funds have been curtailed, or both. None of the 60 or so autonomous institutes have any research agenda that could be considered as evaluative and primary data based. Across these research agencies, it is evident that either they have slowed down or curtailed their research activities recently. The 'autonomous institutes' of course were never visible with primary or even policy research with any transparency. They are being further marginalised. The independent research agencies which acquired institutional stature with credible track records have been more visibly affected recently, signalling decline of research in general and independent research in particular.

Earlier, before 2014, it was the Rajiv Gandhi Foundation which was assigned research projects on priority to do with water, sanitation and public policies despite having no subject experts or field setup to undertake such studies. Now it is the turn of the Vivekananda Foundation. It is busy with research assignments and projects. And there are individuals and groups who are assigned research on a preferential basis irrespective of infrastructure or expertise to undertake dispassionate research. Transparency is questionable in these assignments, in both the cases. That these foundations have direct political affiliations and their activities are talked about as 'party affiliated' has made no difference and their research reaches the larger public. Such a trend and its implications on data reliability are bound to reflect in the context of Global Indexes.

None of the research institutes, both Government and independent ones, have any activities involving academics at any level. Obviously, no fundamental research will remain relevant without continuing research with academics. No research institute can afford to remain professional and transparent without some linkage with academics of higher learning. ICSSR was very active in establishing this linkage decades ago. Even now it assigns academic institutes programmes to do with workshops and seminars, but not so much do with research.

These independent research organisations should perhaps come forward to display their research to remind the country of the status of research in India. Recently, in October 2022, 27 IITs came together and organised an impressive 'fair' to display their research and innovation initiatives. Similar displays of work of independent research organisations will go a long way in reinvigorating the relevance of research in the public domain.

7

REFURBISHING RESEARCH

Rebooting the Research Paradigm

Research in India is no longer a serious pursuit. Independent research, in particular, seems to be in a recession. Research on behaviour, social change, social development and futures is no longer a serious pursuit at any level, not even among academics. This should be of concern to all rational thinking people. Political leaders should realise the implications of this vacuum. It should not become a sign of the decay or decline of governments and governance.

Research in India is in transition, from being an accountable public service to a commercial opportunity or a quid-pro-quo undertaking. This is particularly visible in terms of democracy, development and governance. Research has become subservient to the government of the day. This is problematic. A change of political party or leader in government should not alter research propositions, priorities and the very paradigm of research.

Some of the concerns of the country have been building

over the last century (1920-2022), and research needs to keep consistent track of them. By doing so, it can once again become part of the trajectory of development, democracy and governance. Research requires rejuvenation and integration into academics and governance. It should not lose its unique 'third eye' character and opportunity.

Dr P.C. Mahalanobis envisioned, 70 years ago, that numbers and data should go through rigorous checks and balances so that they don't become subordinate to anyone, particularly bureaucrats. That was why he had positioned research agencies outside the government, or subject to independent scrutiny. He did not foresee that a real threat to the country's statistical system would arise out of political leadership and electoral compulsions. This is the reality now, at all levels.

When facts and figures are doubted, research findings are ridiculed, performance claims are at stake, direction of the economy gets blurred, and so does the political standing of the country. The government's promises and projections are taken with a pinch of salt, threatening the very credibility of the government. All this because data and research is viewed as doubtful or fudged or manipulated. As if there is no rigor in data collection, no validation of research, and no provision for public scrutiny. This situation cannot be ignored for long.

Research is now largely viewed as being either pro or anti-establishment. This gives it a political character, with political interests prevailing. The research pursuit itself has been reduced to ratings of competing interests at the macro level. This leads to what I call a rainbow view of research, where the impact of research is (kept) limited. The research findings are forgotten once the issue is no longer in the news. The short-term outlook of leaders has undermined the potential of research.

Governments are preoccupied with maintaining their own popularity. Numbers seem to have become part of psychological warfare instead of empowering or enlightening citizens and decision makers. An illusionary view of research has taken root, and findings are unquestioned when they are favourable for the day.

That data from credible sources decides the future course has been forgotten or ignored. Instead of the transparency that is the essence of good data, data is now viewed as a commodity, and short-term interests surpass all others. All this needs to be reconsidered and reversed. This cannot happen without the top leadership realising the need for proactive initiatives. The following section outlines some suggestions in order to rejuvenate research in the country.

End Ambiguity

In the more recent years there have been interventions, administrative and political, to destabilise and distort research efforts across all levels and sectors. The New Education Policy (NEP 2020) has added to the ambiguity, particularly in social research and the research culture of the country. The NEP provided for a Research Foundation to bring all research under the control of the Union Government of the day. Instead of decentralising research it has provided for centralisation, as if it has not realised the implications. It is true that research provisions needed to be revamped. But instead of creating another Foundation, the existing ICSSR and UGC, for example, could be revamped and strengthened, and granted autonomy and funding.

The NEP had envisioned a hundred universities with a focus on research. This is good, and much needed. But two years since the policy was announced, nothing is evident on the ground. On the contrary, whatever support was available prior to this policy has been either withdrawn or curtailed as if the government is determined to destabilise research or make research efforts selective. Most of the (over 300) annual awards for research initiatives in academia, for example, were discontinued in October 2022, and these should be revived.

The idea of a National Research Foundation (NRF) should be to explore and expand research opportunities and enhance their credibility. The suggested policy expects research to come under the direct ambit of the Prime Minister instead of liberating research from the shackles of those in power. It suggests that approval of research initiatives needs to be granted at every stage. It also centralises funding for research in both academia and the Ministries. The NEP ignores the existence of the ICSSR and UGC altogether. Instead of minimising political intervention and control in research apparatus, operations and priorities, NEP provides an opposite paradigm which would be a death-knell for research culture and would drive research to a subservient position. The policy needs reconsideration and reversal of the recommendations. It is good that the NRF has not taken off as of 2023. A third eye role of research, on the other hand, is in the interest of the country, its democracy, governance and development. This is not possible unless independent research is encouraged in the country, in academia and outside and the findings are in public domain.

Save Independent Research from Extinction

The uncertain status of independent research in the country is linked to the apprehension that research that exposes the government and debunks their claims will bring down the ire of the authorities. Data is merged or manipulated or even avoided so that what is actually happening will not come to light or not clash with government rhetoric.

The potential of independent research in safeguarding the fundamentals of the country's constitutional provisions should not be lost sight of. Special efforts are required to ensure that research agencies operating outside the Government, independently and professionally, are encouraged to follow certain self-restraints, codes and regulations.

Independent research bodies which are not for profit and which have distinguished themselves professionally over the years should not be equated with commercially operating multinational consultancies which do not adhere to Indian traditions and even regulations. In fact, independent Indian research agencies should be qualified for certain preferential treatment, as the multinationals are given now.

Research Should Be Obligatory

Major national public schemes and programmes of government should be monitored at least twice a year, each time with additional or different parameters. There should be an evaluative study every two or three years, and an impact study every five to ten years. The three different type of studies should be made obligatory and should be provided for with budgetary allocations. These studies should be carried out by an independent agency. The three different levels of study should not be done by the same agency. In fact, it is better if each function is assigned to a different research agency. The local/regional Project Manager should decide a research schedule. A state level nodal agency should suggest protocols for the research agencies.

Project Support Units (PSU) or 'Project Management Support Groups' are used for monitoring and implementation as it suits. This method suits both the consultancy agency (mostly foreign origin) to get into the Ministries (and access their data) and the Government, to get 'supportive research' in return. This amounts to exactly what pioneers like Mahalanobis wanted to avoid. Research and implementation should be separate so that the question of conflict of interest does not arise. The PSU strategy suits both the government and foreign research firms and strengthens their partnerships. The national implications of this situation need to be looked into.

As discussed earlier, with the influx of research agencies into India since the economic reforms, the research scenario has changed. From being independent, they have become part of multinational syndicates. Soon, under the garb of Project Support Units (PSU) or Project Management Support Team (PMST), some of these research agencies operate from within the Ministries directly. Even state governments have adopted this course. Supportive and endorsement research should be distinguished from participatory and independent research. Otherwise it amounts to an extension of deceptive political interests.

Research Should Be Part of Higher Education

Long ago, in the early fifties, 'Planning Forums' in colleges and universities sensitised students to the problems that different sections of population face and how a planning approach helps in addressing them. There are such forums on a few academic campuses today, but nothing of that sort exists on research methodologies. ICSSR is limited to supporting short-term programmes. But more recently with private universities, new hope and new ideas are coming out. In October 2022, 23 IITs came together with a 'fair' to showcase the initiatives and experiments their students and departments had undertaken with research. That was first time research talent was displayed as a fair for the understanding of the concerned public. Colleges should have research data banks or data repositories where any student on campus across disciplines could undertake research on any of the themes they intend to pursue.

Apps

New technology tools need to be part of research academics. This could start with orientation for faculties to acquaint them with new opportunities and challenges. ICCSR could coordinate this, particularly in terms of new software and Apps, for monitoring, analysing and appraising public policies.

Restore Research Institutions, Save Them from Extinction

Research organisations of all kinds should have legal existence, be accountable and have social responsibility of their own. And above all, they should have self-respect and maintain research standards.

Individual research projects should go through 'ethical scrutiny' as a part of social responsibility. This is to ensure that research is not conducted for misleading purposes or for the advantage of any individual or group, or be unconcerned with possible disadvantage to any particular section or region through the research outcome.

Research today is often carried out to exploit an opportunity for political or commercial advantage. This trend needs to be restrained. Responsible and credible research organisations should not succumb to biased or supportive research. Instances of planting 'findings' or data as research results has become a practice among unscrupulous elements and collaborative news media. Certain periodic measures are required by civil society, ICSSR and similar public bodies to expose such contentious tendencies. Research that is put into the public domain should pass through public scrutiny of one kind or another as to the procedures followed to arrive at the findings.

Sponsorship, Transparency and Access

A DFID report in September 2011 on Social Science Research in India concluded that 'lack of proper institutional support' is a factor leading to 'variable research quality'.

International multilateral agencies like the Word Bank, ADB, DFID, CIDA, USAID, NORD, UN agencies, etc., who have been sponsoring and commissioning research in India since 1990, have reduced their research activities in the last decade. There is no evidence that independent research and evaluation continues as a condition for lending policies.

Concern about 'donor influence' on research and priorities

should be welcomed. Some ICSSR reviews, by Chatterjee in 2002 and Papola in 2010 have examined the adverse influence of such research. In fact, some scholars even observed the 'negative implications for academic quality'. Even an IDRC round table made such observations as early as in 2008. These are public documents. Yet they were not taken note of for their implications for the research environment in the country and for public policy making.

Most research remains confidential or confined to a few privileged and interested parties. The real role of research depends on the findings being made available to stakeholders. Only then is there a chance of it being effectively utilised and prompting behavioural change. In fact, there should be special efforts to ensure that research findings are in the public domain and that there is transparency on all aspects of research, particularly publicly funded research and research that aims at influencing larger public policies.

Syndicated research allows more stakeholders to avail of the research instead of research findings remaining confined to those who can afford them or to a privileged few. Syndicated research should be promoted, so that research reports to do with public policies and services can be shared or be available for subscription to anyone. Thereby, findings and analysis would be available simultaneously and at least cost. This has helped many enterprises and has helped de-monopolise the markets and grip of multinationals on research more specifically. I hoped years ago that ICSSR would initiate such an approach to equalise access to research data and findings. Research should not be limited to a few. The more who are aware of research the better it is, particularly social research and publicly funded research. It was Dr Vikram Sarabhai's idea that ORG adopt a syndicate approach and that was how it made available its Store Audit, Pharma Audit, Readership Surveys, etc. as syndicate reports in the early 1970s, simultaneously to all. This facilitated the spread of research sensitivity in the country. The idea disappeared with the influx of foreign research agencies. It is time to revive syndicated research on public schemes across the country.

All-out Efforts in Academics

Independent research is not possible overnight or even in a five-year electoral cycle. It needs to be cultivated among academics, civil society, and policy making systems and has to become built into democracy, development and governance systems. This is a compulsion for sustaining good governance without compromising development and democracy. News media as well as civil society needs to be sensitised about credibility of research and its implications for reliability.

Open forums which cultivate sustained discussion of research are disappearing. Even formal media like EPW (*Economic & Political Weekly*) which promotes independent research is on the decline or repositioning itself. Open forums are essential for the credibility of policy research in particular.

Academic platforms are no longer actively engaged in research activities, nor do they provide critical forums for discussion of research as they used to. It is the sensitivities of academic faculties which sustain such an interest. Neither the Indian Science Congress nor any of the Associations of various academic disciplines like the Indian Sociology Association or Political Science or Anthropology Association are seen debating about the status of research, or the pros and cons of different methodologies. Even Economic Associations which were very active in earlier years debating procedures and methodologies are no longer engaged at the same level. Without restoring the sanctity of such professional and academic forums, we cannot expect to restore either the credibility or independence of research.

Even in academic syllabi, research as a discipline is being edged out, no matter what is proclaimed in formal policies. Research methods and analytics are reduced to software opportunities. A holistic view where understanding of linkages is inculcated is missing from higher education. Without this, concepts or theory building make no sense nor do they sustain knowledge building and the intellect.

Governments are more often discouraging of or discriminative against the fundamentals of research. When a new regime comes into power, they tend to use extant research selectively or start from scratch.

Research is viewed now as the hand-maid of control and command interests. This leads to persuasive or consensus-building research and homogenising efforts. Because of this clear set of government priorities, the greater the extent of the government's involvement, the lower the credibility of data and research. Instead of employing professional field investigators, the governments tend to fiddle with data and mess with reliability or compatibility aspects, which amounts to erosion of the very credibility of the country itself in terms of data and research.

Academics tend to remain outside the loop of applied research in the country. Despite courses on statistics, research methodology and the compulsions of project reports at the postgraduate level, it has not sparked any new ideas, or helped consolidate the research status of universities, even as syndicates. Universities claim research strength without actually doing much and with no new skills acquired by students even at post graduate level.

As the DFID review pointed out in 2011, the 'university administration is not research friendly and there is no incentive structure.' The review also stated that 'a great deal of policy research simply does not enter the public domain.' There has been no change since then, and it needs to be addressed.

In 2021, in *The Third Eye of Governance* I suggested various multipronged initiatives as safeguards to ensure that research fulfils its potential. First, state authorities should periodically reiterate the role and relevance of, and their support for, research for public policies and for assessing outcomes. Second, some transparent and independent regulatory mechanism is desirable in the research architecture and, particularly, self-disciplinary obligations should be promoted. Third, from time-to-time professional organisations, including academics, should undertake sensitivity building activities revolving around statistics, data and the way they are presented in various public news media. And, further, research methodologies should be multi-faceted.

This is what Amitabh Kant, Indian representative at the G20 meet in December 2022 suggested, and proposed 'safeguards against data misuse'. In the government, all such measures which are taken need to be indicated in each case. This should include responsibility for misuse of data inside and outside the government.

A Culture of Enquiry

As discussed, research endeavours in India need to be revived. Can a nation afford to deprive itself of the serious advantages of research? When the country is pursuing the aim of good governance, the government should have nothing to do with demoralising or curbing research culture. The result otherwise will tell both at home and abroad. It is rather an imperative that research efforts are restored to their proper stature and their utilisation is evident in policy framing. It is high time that the country realises the relevance of research at all levels and contexts.

However, just realisation is not enough. It has to be that research is not superfluous but an essential part of the national endeavour towards a better future. This means that research inputs are more pertinent than advertising and publicity. This cannot happen without serious and sequential correctives, promotional measures and initiatives by the governments, academics, and in the civic society. Only then can we participate on the global stage and improve the situation in terms of development, stature, welfare and governance. Introspective initiatives at the level of individual research institutions and sectors like academia and industry would speed up the corrective course.

Reinstate Research As a Spring Board

Research in the country regains its relevance and becomes a national culture only when viewed holistically. The country is fortunate that there are a host of apex research bodies in different sectors like CSIR, ICAR, ICMR, ICSSR, NCERT, etc. and institutes of higher education like the universities,

IIMs, IITs, etc. They all should be assured that research is supported and allowed objective and professional research opportunities. Such a message has to be clear. All the independent research outfits catering to the markets, industry and the interests of civil society like CSDS, CSE, CMS, etc., should be reviewed by a high level composite committee, to determine how research across sectors can flourish as a national strength and unleash their potential to improve the stature of the country.

Research culture has to originate from academia and percolate across media. How much do we see that now? Sadly, compared to a few decades ago, the decline of research in academia is evident across disciplines. Exploration and enquiry has to be inherent in the curriculum. It was as a part of the requirements of graduation degrees that research began to be pursued. Today, both teaching methods and syllabus requirements do not allow any experimentation with research methodologies.

It is high time that academic institutes are strengthened with a focus on research as a discipline. Research methods need to be reinstated as a part of course requirements.

In a good initiative, in 2018 the Government declared 20 universities as 'eminent to excel in research'. Nearly half of the ones named were outside the Government's control. But, a year later, the NEP envisaged '100 universities with focus on research'. A quick analysis of what is actually happening in the universities since then reveals the further decline in the quality of research, even in the requirements of PhD theses. And more than one third of faculty positions continue to be vacant in most universities. The UGC (University Grants

Commission) which reviews, sets norms and funds too has been in a confused state with regard to encouraging research and upholding research standards. Its recent guidelines, for example, on PhD theses, faculty appointments and procedures for research keep research under the bureaucratic thumb or political grip. ICSSR and UGC should revive courses on research and research methodologies and review the research requirements for PhD and MPhil degrees. Courses on enquiry, data, analytics and research should be introduced earlier. There are already some schools like the International School of Hyderabad (on ICRISAT campus), which has been teaching children about research from the 8th class, exploring basic concepts of enquiry.

Admission into social science courses has declined recently. The social sciences include a number of disciplines, each with its own theoretical foundations: Geography, Sociology, Political Science, Psychology, Anthropology and Economics. But for the requirement of the competitive civil service exam, anthropology would have seen a further decline. Admissions to commerce, computer, IT, law and personal development subjects, on the other hand, have increased.

It is heartening to see that private universities like Ashoka, Jindal, Wipro, Galgotias, etc., have demonstrated how independent research could be revived, and are rejuvenating academic standards. It is also encouraging that the number of patents received by private universities has shown an increase. IIT Delhi has set up a School of Public Policy with the assistance of the Tata Trust and such initiatives could be hotspots of research in academia.

The study of futures should be part of academic courses. This requires an understanding of the linkage between variables, and which obviously requires ongoing research to look beyond a five or ten years perspective. Future studies are not being shared and are not in public domain. TIFAC (The Technology, Information, Forecasting and Assessment Council) is no longer visible today. Today, it is election to election concerns that determine research priorities.

In a proactive initiative in November 2022, UGC eased the eligibility qualifications for PhDs in universities. Anyone who has completed a four-year degree, including working professionals, can enrol for a PhD now. UGC rightly suggested that half of the syllabus should be 'research methodology'. But it did nothing to suggest what or how 'high quality research' could be pursued. In fact, the courses and number of hours spent on research methodology have been reduced. Filling academic vacancies should be far more of a priority than enrolling more PhD candidates, as the employment opportunities for PhDs are on the decline. How increasing the numbers of PhDs is going to better the standards or even credibility of research is not evident. The general impression is that the new regulations will further diminish academic rigour, particularly research standards, and priorities of concern. Also, chances of students' early exit before graduation have increased. There has been no suggested measure to increase transparency in research. However, discretionary opportunities for the government to intervene have been increased. Nothing has been done to address the shortage of research faculty across academia. In Delhi University and its colleges, for example, 6000 faculty positions are vacant and temporary ones are in position, particularly for research positions. This practice alone is a damper on research quality.

In 2020, India accounted for only 4.5 per cent of total research papers in the world, though it accounts for 12 per cent of the global faculty pool. And yet the requirement for publication or presentation of research theses has been withdrawn instead of promoting rigour in that requirement.

Our early nation builders envisioned the dangers of the research apparatus coming under the bureaucracy which is responsible for implementation of government schemes, plans and policies. The way the New Research Foundation has been outlined in the NEP of 2020 implies bringing research under a new 'academic bureaucracy', exactly what our early leaders hoped to avoid.

Safeguards Should Be Inbuilt

As no subject expert could be unbiased altogether, research too can be biased. Bias in research could be there knowingly and unknowingly. It could creep in at different points, levels and phases of research. Being aware or cautious and taking into account and acknowledging any such bias or limitation is critical. Transparency in terms of the process, and checks and balance mechanisms provide objectivity to research. Research by its very nature implies a certain liberal view though it may yield a reactionary outlook and outcomes. Researchers have a responsibility to be concerned about any biases inherent at any point and should consciously overcome them. Acknowledging particular biases is the least one expects and, in fact, should be obligatory for policy research. An ethical review by an independent panel of stake holders would minimise these fears. An Ethical Review Board should be constituted for certain critical departments and research services.

Designated Funding and Budget

Hardly 0.25 per cent of the GDP is spent on social and policy research. Even in the context of flagship programs involving large sections of the population, very little of the budget is spent on research. Overall, the budget for R&D research has been much below two per cent. In comparison, private sector or marketing companies with a concern for outcomes spend more than 10 per cent of their turnover on research.

For social sector projects, governments in India spend more on publicity and advertising than on research of any kind. In fact, not even half of the publicity budget is spent for research even where it should be a priority and even a compulsion. This present trend should be urgently reversed in order to achieve national development goals.

The budget allocation of Governments/Ministries for data, research, monitoring and evaluation has declined over the recent years. What is allocated remains unused or used for something else in the name of research. This practice too needs to be reviewed and reversed. Budget should be specifically provided for research and also actually used for it. A certain percentage of project funding should be earmarked for research as an obligatory requirement at various stages of implementation of public schemes. Budgets should be outcome-oriented and show evidence sensitivity. This is possible only with research, particularly independent research. Research by academic faculties too should be concerned with these aspects.

All this is possible only when the overall budget and expenditure on R&D in the country is more than two per cent of GDP. But outlays on R&D have come down from

0.8 per cent a decade ago to 0.65 per cent of GDP. The NRF has raised hopes of reversing that trend. It remains to be seen whether it will succeed.

Electoral Compulsions Need Moderation

Electoral compulsions have directly affected social and policy research in India, particularly in the last two decades. This has limited the scope of evidence-based research. Political leaders' concern with image-building has led to supportive or endorsing research. Preoccupation with poll surveys and jugglery with percentages is sustaining that trend. Electoral compulsions are hostile to independent research and a reflective methodology as well as rigor in the data and field work and objectivity in analyses and fairness in report writing. This cannot change overnight. It has to become a continuing concern. Restoration of trust in research is not possible without sensitising the public. Independent researchers can help in promoting this sensitivity and seriousness.

Politics and political leaders' involvement in conducting research on public issues, even remotely, erodes the credibility of the research. But interactions with them before formulating research studies, particularly on massive public schemes, would be useful. Collaborative studies, or those carried out by consortia, should be transparent and state this upfront.

Global Indexes and the Credibility of Research

As discussed earlier, the way the global indexes rank India signals the lack of credibility of research sources in India.

The Government is ambiguous about global indexes. Some are taken seriously and many more are abused or rebutted.

India should either ignore them all or take an active interest in proactive measures to improve our rank. A lasting solution to faring better in any global index is in performing well on vital indicators of development and, equally important, to restore reliability and consistency of data and research and reinstate transparency and independent research.

The Government should form a group to look into the various indexes and advise on how to deal professionally with them, and involve academics and independent institutes. There is currently no evidence of the government addressing India's global index rankings adequately, or critically appraising the methodologies. A group of independent experts, of which we have many, should look into the methodology and data used for individual indexes like democracy, human development, environmental performance and the like.

NITI Aayog, on An All-round Mission

NITI Aayog has an ambitious and all-round role, including data collection, curation, assessment and evaluative research. Its endeavour appears focussed on mobilising 'supportive research'. It needs transparency in its functioning, so that its expertise gets the standing it deserves. It tries to be the nucleus of research in the country on its own terms, without any reflective voices in its team. NITI Aayog should have a consultative forum for data reliability and authenticity and for issues to do with periodic monitoring and evaluation.

Pilot First

National schemes, and even state-level schemes, should first be experimented with on various parameters and scaled up with modifications after a pilot study at the micro level. Research offers objective insights in this process and ensures better implementation and realisation of the objectives at the macro level. Pilots should be a prerequisite for certain complex flagship programmes. Pilots should end with research scrutiny of both the process and the outcome.

Advocacy research is not necessarily by lobbies of self-interested groups but could be for the larger good. In fact, many campaigns to do with social development may evoke adverse responses even though they are based on facts, figures and analysis. This distinction between the two is what research should make clear and sensitise the implementing agencies and stake holders. Special efforts are required towards such public sensitivity drives.

Participatory research is no longer in the spotlight today. It is time-consuming, requires far more infrastructure and costs more than sample surveys. Sample surveys, using sampling methodologies, have become more often relied upon, including by individual global indexes. Many today are phone-based interviews, not face-to-face at the grassroots. Many social development and behavioural change issues benefit from participatory research. Independent social policy research is on an extinction course as if it is a hindrance or 'cost burden'.

Less Government, More Credibility

The focus of research gets lost when it is conducted at the macro level. This is particularly the case when it is Government-driven. The data, evaluation and research findings become less credible. This is known globally. The greater the independence from the Government and even corporates, the higher the credibility of the research.

Many research and training institutes were set up by Union and State Governments as autonomous bodies under the Societies Act with either the Minister or Secretary of the concerned Ministries as the chairman. In reality they operate as a part of the Ministry. As a result, these institutes are neither autonomous nor of the Government. This situation, which has lasted 30 years or more, needs a review. A domain subject expert should be the chairman and the executive should operate professionally even if it depends on the Ministry for financial support. The ambiguity should end so that these institutes can be proactive.

Research At State Levels

Earlier, most research, basic and policy, took place at the Union level and state governments used the same data. But now states are generating their own data, based on different field surveys with their own modalities, often with conflicting methodologies and outcomes. This is a new phenomenon taking away from the credibility of research. In the process often there is a difference between the data of states and the union and even in the definitions used. With states under the rule of different political parties, the use of different definitions and data adds to confusion. This is a serious issue also because both the union and the state data are viewed as politically massaged. Also, in this process, state governments tend to use 'their own' local people for 'field surveys', instead of independent or trained investigators. Such 'surveys' further complicate the issues. This needs to be addressed.

Advertising Is No Surrogate for Research

The impression one gets is that perhaps the governments consider advertising and publicity as better than research and evaluation. Why else do they continue to pour money into advertising and publicity, while reducing budgets for research. This trend should be reversed.

Market research, opinion research and election surveys influence the way policy and evaluation research takes place in the country. The agencies conducting these studies are the same ones who are engaged in other applied research. Not only the same field investigators, even the same methodologies are relied upon for behavioural and social studies. These methodologies serve temporary interests over longer term ones. The Market Research Association has certain codes which it expects its members to observe. This is good self-discipline among independent research agencies. Both the government and news media should encourage those who are members of such associations. The Advertising Standards Council of India (ASCI) is another agency which has set a good example in the country for standards. As an independent body of stakeholders, it has become a model for public services, particularly for research on public policies. It has proactive initiatives for good practices. Such an organisation on social policy research and consultancy operations should be active also. The government could take the initiative in encouraging such an outfit.

Vacancies As Never Before: Many national research institutes are without a director. These higher level positions including at educational institutes require government clearance. In many cases the process of selection gets derailed by secretary level officers of the government controlling those institutes for a variety of reasons. These vacancies need to be filled as soon as possible, and in an unbiased way.

Advocacy Research: ASER, ADR and NFHS are examples of research services whose periodic independent reports play a significant role in the state of public affairs and policies. The NFHS report, although it is coordinated by a government-controlled autonomous institute, the field work is undertaken by private research organisations. There are a few other such examples: the CMS report on corruption, CES report on Environment, Citizen Card of Public Affairs Centre, India Today's annual review and rankings of states with MDRA as research partner. These efforts deserve recognition for undertaking studies on contentious and complex issues. They demonstrate what difference independent research agencies with social obligations could make. This reminds us of the potential for advocacy research that independent research organisations could undertake on long-standing issues. Advocacy research need not be seen as the prerogative of 'lobbistics', as it is largely viewed. It has a huge positive role to play.

Outsourcing and Responsibility

The outsourcing of research studies of public schemes should not be on a least cost basis (L-1). Social and policy research should have different criteria for selecting the research agency. Non-profit research agencies engaged in independent research no longer have equal opportunity. This amounts to encouraging research to become 'commercial' or as an arrangement that is more likely to suit the political interests of those in government.

To qualify to bid for research for the government, research agencies are expected to have a high capital amount. This amount is usually so high that hardly any Indian agency would qualify. Even the earnest money deposit or bank guarantee (until the close of the project) requirement is high, as if to disqualify Indian research outfits even to bid for government research projects. The weightage given in selecting the research agency is to the disadvantage of local research agencies. 'Quality Cost Based Support' (QCBS) and 'Least Cost System' (L-1) methods were introduced two decades ago, even for social research assignments. Standardised evaluation criteria are not used, even for research on the SDGS (with 17 goals to achieve). There is no evidence that these procedures of government have made any difference in the quality and reliability of research so procured (from mostly foreign or multinational research corporates).

Given the volume of research ideally needed in the context of nearly 1000 national schemes of Rs.15 lac crore expenditure, we should have a transparent National Policy for research or data and for baseline and evaluative requirements.

Research agencies, to prequalify for research on public policies, should have been registered with the minimum prequalifying infrastructure. And such a registered agency should further be qualified to conduct a particular study in terms of local infrastructure and capabilities. Foreign-affiliated or based research outfits should indicate their association or affiliations outside the country, and their origins should be evident from the registration.

UN bodies, the World Bank and such other aid agencies had a condition earlier that all aided projects should have research at two or three levels or phases of the project. This should not become a mere formality. It should be an obligation, whose fulfilment is evident.

Research priorities and assignments should always be backed by a small research committee (formal or informal) at district level and at state levels (of 3-5 members). At least one member should be from civil society, one from academia and one from the executive (retired or serving) and at least one should be a woman. Such a research advisory committee should be a standing body.

A team of independent experts from outside the government should review, once in five years, the nodal research agencies operating under different missions/Ministries. Those include ICMR, CSIR, ICAR, NCERT, ICSSR, UGC and the like. Transparency and methodology issues should be included in their review terms, apart from report content.

Lessons from Industry/Corporate Research

What the industry and corporates spend on research is far more than what the governments spend on research. They use research and also benefit from it commensurately. Their research modalities, in fact, offer far more insights than government-sponsored research. Most market-driven or consumer research is confined to commercial use and most of it is not available in the public domain or shared with others. But even the governments of late are using research more often, but covertly, as if it is meant only for control or for vigilance or for intelligence on citizens and civil society.

Reviving the research institutes which already exist should be an immediate task of the government. This would take the form of allocations and disbursement of funds, and allowing them to function professionally, in pursuit of larger public interests. They should be eased out of the clutches of the bureaucracy in such a way that they could function competently and take proactive initiatives as well.

Recent proliferation of data, data bases and apps have dramatically changed the scope and potential of research. The very paradigm and practices of research are changing. As we have seen, a quantitative outlook has taken over, not qualitative concerns or long-range change implications, which means immediate effects, not impact, has become the concern and priority. Surrogates and top of the mind recalls have become the prevailing methodologies, along with projection and simulation. It is the interests of control and centralisation that dictate. Now Artificial Intelligence (AI) is further changing the scope of research. With governments bringing in legislative initiatives and interventions with instruments like Aadhar, Voter Card, online use of data bases, digitalisation, 'Control room' criticality has taken over the research framework. Social change and behavioural studies have made privacy notional and illusionary. We need different research methodologies with far more transparency and credibility. What is needed more than 'centralisation' is transparency in formulation and managing the data systems and data base services.

REFERENCES

Chapter 1

- https://books.google.co.in/books/about/Social_Science_Research_in_India.html?id=NBXltAEACAAJ&source=kp_book_description&redir_esc=y
- https://www.amazon.in/Social-Science-Research-India-Institutions/dp/8171888445
- https://www.amazon.in/Social-Science-Research-India-Policies/dp/0199474419
- https://www.flipkart.com/third-eye-governance-rise-populism-decline-social-research/p/itm46957fc0c573f
- *The Hindu*, June 11, 2022, https://www.thehindu.com/sci-tech/energy-and-environment/explained-why-is-india-ranked-at-the-bottom-of-the-2022-environmental-performance-index/article65511480.ece
- *The Telegraph*, January 5, 2022, https://www.telegraphindia.com/india/ugc-stops-research-projects-due-to-lack-of-funds-from-centre/cid/1846232)
- https://www.krctimes.com/news/india-climbs-40th-rank-in-global-innovation-index-of-wipo/
- *The Hindu*, 27-9-2022, https://www.thehindu.com/news/national/centre-to-reduce-number-of-awards-given-for-scientific-research/article65939232.ece

- *Indian Express*, Oct 12, 2022, https://indianexpress.com/article/cities/delhi/in-memo-to-staff-aiims-says-get-health-minister-nod-to-invite-dignitaries-8203363/
- Arunachalam, S. 2008. Social science research in South Asia: An analysis of the published journal literature. New Delhi: IDRC.
- Chatterjee, P. 2002. Institutional context of social science research in South Asia. *Economic and Political Weekly* August 31: 3604-3612.
- Government of India. 2011. Report of the committee constituted by the Government of India to review the functioning of ICSSR. New Delhi: Ministry of Human Resource Development.
- ICSSR. 2007. Restructuring the Indian Council of Social Science Research, Report of the Fourth Review Committee. New Delhi: ICSSR
- Mathur, 2009. Policy research organizations in South Asia. New Delhi: IDRC
- Papola, T.S. 2010. Social science research in globalizing India: Historical developments and recent trends. New Delhi: ISID Working Paper.
- Dr N. Bhaskara Rao, *The Third Eye of Governance*, Speaking Tiger, 2021
- Dr N. Bhaskara Rao, *Sustainable Good Governance, Development and Democracy*, SAGE Publications, 2019

Chapter 2

- Prabhash Ranjan, 'Still a Developing Country', *The Hindu*, October 31, 2019, https://www.thehindu.com/opinion/op-ed/still-a-developing-country/article29834940.ece
- Sriman Narayan Agarwal, *The Gandhian Plan of Economic Development for India*, Palala Press, September 2015.

- J.C. Kumarappa, *Gandhian Economic Thought*, Sarva Seva Sangh Prakashan (Varanasi), 2010.
- https://www.exoticindiaart.com/product/audiovideo/discovery-of-india-bharat-ek-khoj-set-of-18-dvds-with-book-ict199/?sitecurrency=INR&gclid=CjwKCAiAr4GgBhBFEiwAgwORrW5LcK6OqoFNgNGECLTRXlMRYmSshim-QEWqJXfxkfOJJmBnE-E-mFxo CLlwQAvD_BwE
- *Hindustan Times*, January 15, 2023, https://www.hindustantimes.com/india-news/a-deep-rumble-cracks-what-ensued-in-joshimath-on-january-2-101673717521 348.html
- N. Bhaskara Rao (ed.), 'India 2021', ORG, 1985
- *Business Standard*, December 30, 2022, https://www.business-standard.com/article/opinion/lunch-with-bs-g20-is-about-thinking-and-acting-big-says-amitabh-kant-122123000800_1.html, https://twitter.com/BajpaiKanti/status/1609245737610805250?s=08
- https://www.washingtonpost.com/news/worldviews/wp/2017/10/24/einstein-scribbled-his-theory-of-happiness-in- place-of-a-tip-it-just-sold-for-more-than-1-million/
- https://www.netajisubhasbose.org/post/subhas-chandra-bose-and-meghnad-saha
- https://archivepmo.nic.in/abv/speech-details.php?nodeid=9106
- https://www.thehindu.com/todays-paper/2023-03-13/th_delhi/articleG3NAVTQ9D-2344959.ece
- https://www.thehindu.com/data/data-three-government-surveys-debunk-swachh-bharats-100-odf-claim/undefined

Chapter 3

- *Livemint*, June 8, 2022, https://www.livemint.com/news/india/india-ranks-lowest-in-environmental-performance-index-2022-11654594336783.html

- *The Hindu*, 16 Oct. 2022, https://www.thehindu.com/news/national/explained-understanding-the-global-hunger-index/article66019051.ece
- *The Print*, November 30, 2022, https://theprint.in/india/desi-global-minority-index-puts-india-at-top-says-caa-protest-notable-sign-of-status-of-muslims/1242087/
- https://www.geeksforgeeks.org/indias-ranking-in-different-index-2022/
- https://www.hindustantimes.com/technology/denmark-tops-digital-quality-of-life-global-index-where-does-india-stand-101663042686266.html
- *Indian Express*, Oct. 14, 2019, https://indianexpress.com/article/world/2019-nobel-prize-for-economics-awarded-to-abhijit-banerjee-esther-duflo-and-michael-kremer/
- *The Times of India*, Jan 31, 2023, https://timesofindia.indiatimes.com/india/president-droupadi-murmu-in-her-1st-joint-address-to-parliament-full-speech/articleshow/97480764.cms
- IndiaSpend, May 2, 2023, '34 Million or 373 Million: Do We Know How Many In India Are Poor?', https://www.indiaspend.com/poverty/34-million-or-373-million-do-we-know-how-many-in-india-are-poor-861467#.ZFTfURP9ttB.whatsapp
- CNBCTV18, Jan 16, 2023, https://www.cnbctv18.com/economy/its-all-about-how-india-continues-to-be-one-bright-spot-in-the-global-economy-interview-with-parameswaran-iyer-ceo-niti-aayog-at-davos-15678721.htm
- *The Print*, 14 September, 2022, https://theprint.in/opinion/why-indias-democracy-ranking-should-be-taken-with-a-grain-of-salt/1127765/
- *Hindustan Times*, Sep 09, 2022, https://www.hindustantimes.com/india-news/india-slips-one-rank-in-un-human-index-rating-101662662038125.html

- *Hindustan Times*, April 17, 2021, https://www.hindustantimes.com/india-news/govt-seeks-details-of-parameters-to-improve-india-s-ranking-on-global-democracy-index-101618608140311.html
- CNN, August 28, 2022, https://edition.cnn.com/2022/08/28/us/eric-liu-american-democracy-resilient-cec/index.html
- *SSRN Electronic Journal*, January 2019, https://www.researchgate.net/publication/334033474_Analysis_of_Social_Science_Research_in_India_A_Mapping_Report
- *The Wire*, August 17, 2021; https://thewire.in/government/modi-law-minister-disallow-rajya-sabha-question-democracy-index
- *India Today*, May 19, 2003 | UPDATED: Jun 25, 2012, https://www.indiatoday.in/magazine/cover-story/story/20030519-best-states-to-live-in-india-goa-delhi-rank-higher-than-states-like-gujarat-maharashtra-792923-2003-05-18
- *The Wire*, July 13, 2021, https://thewire.in/education/india-world-class-universities-higher-education
- *Livemint*, November 22, 2022, https://www.livemint.com/news/india/eac-questions-india-rankings-by-3-global-bodies-calls-it-arbitrary-11669139236759.html
- *The Wire*, July 28, 2023, https://thewire.in/government/ks-james-nfhs-modi- government-data-sets-iips
- *The Hindu Business Line*, April 3, 2023, https://www.thehindubusinessline.com/money-and-banking/indias-global-happiness-index-rank-should-be-48-not-126-sbi-ecowrap/article66693946.ece
- *The Wire*, April 14, 2023, https://thewire.in/economy/imf-downgraded-india-growth-slow-domestic-consumption-says-top-official

Source of global index referred

- https://en.wikipedia.org/wiki/Democracy_Index
- https://www.livemint.com/news/india/eac-questions-india-rankings-by-3-global-bodies-calls-it-arbitrary-11669139236759.html
- https://www.v-dem.net/documents/29/V-dem_democracy report2023_lowres.pdf
- https://freedomhouse.org/country/india/freedom-world/2023
- https://www.globalhungerindex.org/india.html
- https://www.thehindu.com/news/national/india-ranks-107-out-of-121-countries-on-global-hunger-index/article 66010797.ece
- https://www.undp.org/india/press-releases/india-ranks-132-human-development-index-global-development-stalls
- https://ccpi.org/country/ind/
- https://thewire.in/environment/india-ranked-in-top-5-countries-on-global-climate-performance-index-power-ministry
- https://epi.yale.edu/downloads/epi2022report06062022.pdf
- https://epi.yale.edu/epi-results/2022/component/epi
- https://www.cato.org/sites/cato.org/files/2023-01/human-freedom-index-2022.pdf
- https://www.fraserinstitute.org/studies/human-freedom-index-2022
- https://www.transparency.org/en/cpi/2022
- https://www.deccanherald.com/national/world-press-freedom-index-india-slips-to-161st-rank-pak-afghanistan-improve-to-150-152-respectively-1215232.html
- https://www.imd.org/centers/wcc/world-competitiveness-center/rankings/world-competitiveness-ranking/

- https://impact.economist.com/sustainability/project/food-security-index/
- https://www.businesstoday.in/latest/story/come-to-bengaluru-and-see-s-jaishankar-rejects-indias-ranking-in-world-happiness-index-2023-375036-2023-03-27
- https://www.thehindu.com/news/national/india-ranks-135-out-of-146-in-global-gender-gap-index/article65636167.ece
- https://economictimes.indiatimes.com/news/economy/indicators/india-breaks-into-top-40-innovative-nations-ranking/articleshow/94540108.cms?from=mdr
- https://worldjusticeproject.org/rule-of-law-index/country/2022/India/
- http://www.ncgg.org.in/sites/default/files/lectures-document/1_1.pdf
- https://www.gfmag.com/global-data/economic-data/world-inequality-ranking
- https://www.heritage.org/index/pdf/2022/book/2022_IndexOfEconomicFreedom_FINAL.pdf
- https://www.oxfamindia.org/press-release/2022-crii-india-moves-six-places-inequality-index-continues-be-among-lowest-performers-health
- https://www.aninews.in/news/world/asia/india-ranks-1-among-110-nations-for-inclusivity-measures-towards-religious-minorities-report20230206235039/
- https://www.business-standard.com/india-news/india-falls-6-spots-to-rank-144-in-passport-index-2023-all-you-must-know-123033000322_1.html
- https://affairscloud.com/arton-capitals-passport-index-2023-india-ranked-144-with-mobility-score-70-uae-ranks-1st/
- https://www.cnbctv18.com/india/social-progress-index-2022-full-list-of-states-puducherry-tops-jharkhand-bihar-rank-low-15462981.htm

- https://chandlergovernmentindex.com/country-rankings/
- https://www.financialexpress.com/industry/india-ranks-42nd-out-of-55-nations-in-global-ip-index/2992309/
- https://www.timesnownews.com/mirror-now/in-focus/most-liveable-city-list-2022-check-delhi-mumbai-indias-city-rank-in-the-list-article-92430563
- https://www.visualcapitalist.com/cp/ranking-countries-by-digital-quality-of-life-2022/
- https://economictimes.indiatimes.com/news/economy/policy/ease-of-doing-business-govt-working-on-to-reduce-compliance-issues-says-official/articleshow/92705974.cms?from=mdr
- https://www.kidsrights.org/research/kidsrights-index/
- https://www.visionofhumanity.org/wp-content/uploads/2022/06/GPI-2022-web.pdf
- https://www.economicsandpeace.org/wp-content/uploads/2023/03/GTI-2023-web-270323.pdf
- https://www.imo-official.org/year_country_r.aspx?year=2022
- https://www.usnews.com/news/best-countries/india
- https://www.insead.edu/sites/default/files/assets/dept/fr/gtci/GTCI-2022-report.pdf
- https://www.livemint.com/economy/india-jumps-6-places-in-world-bank-s-logistics-performance-index-2023-11682517293546.html

Chapter 4

- *The Wire*, Oct 14, 2022, https://thewire.in/agriculture/farmer-suicides-ncrb-data-versus-pau-data
- *Dainik Bhaskar*, August 2022, https://mobile.twitter.com/churumuri/status/1562281112709128192?cxt=HHwWgICjpaGZq64rAAAA

- *Hindustan Times*, March 20, 2014, https://www.hindustantimes.com/india/with-malice-towards-one-and-all-best-of-khushwant-s-columns/story-YlA14F1dFw3js1Gh14ZoJK.html
- *The Wire*, August 15, 2022, https://thewire.in/government/india-75-its-time-to-take-stock-of-promises-that-modi-said-would-be-achieved-by-2022
- *IndiaSpend*, May 2, 2023, https://www.indiaspend.com/poverty/34-million-or-373-million-do-we-know-how-many-in-india-are-poor-861467
- *The Wire*, January 18, 2022, https://thewire.in/government/a-failed-attempt-to-create-an-equally-sanitary-india
- *The Hindu*, December 29, 2022, https://www.thehindu.com/news/national/modi-government-promised-to-double-farm-income-by-2022-but-it-has-only-come-down-congress/undefined
- *Hindustan Times*, July 28, 2018, https://www.hindustantimes.com/india-news/by-2022-every-indian-will-have-a-house-promises-pm-modi/story-z2ZAADfVfDemFWItiM1oXI.html
- *The Hindu*, July 12, 2022, https://www.thehindu.com/news/national/centre-has-no-data-on-child-labour-since-nclp-was-merged-with-samagra-shiksha-abhiyan/article65631877.ece
- *The Wire*, August 04, 2022, https://thewire.in/rights/ground-report-even-after-75-years-of-independence-manual-scavenging-continues-unabated-in-india
- *The Wire*, August 30, 2022, https://thewire.in/women/crimes-against- women-rape-cases-india-2021-ncrb-data
- *Down To Earth*, March 16, 2018, https://www.downtoearth.org.in/news/105th-indian-science-congress/ extend-research-from-labs-to-the-land-modi-at-105th-indian-science-congress-59933

Chapter 5

- *The Wire*, December 9, 2022, https://livewire.thewire.in/campus/union-government-discontinues-manf-scholarship-for-minority-communities/
- https://digitalcommons.unl.edu/cgi/viewcontent.cgi?article=7112&context=libphilprac
- https://tribal.nic.in/downloads/TRI/Guidelines/ListofTRIs.pdf
- https://prcpatna.in/list-prc-india.php
- Dr N. Bhaskara Rao, 'Sustainable Good Governance, Development and Democracy', SAGE Publications, 2019, https://www.amazon.com/Sustainable-Good-Governance-Development-Democracy/dp/9352808118
- Dr N. Bhaskara Rao & G.N.S. Raghvan, 'Social Effects of Mass Media in India', Gyan Publishing House, 1996, https://www.snapdeal.com/product/social-effects- of-mass-media/670791874487
- *The Indian Express*, July 11, 2023, https://indianexpress.com/article/opinion/columns/criticism-of-sample-surveys-is-misplaced-their-data-differ-from-census-count-because-definitions-are-different-8822347/

Chapter 6

- https://orgindia.com/
- https://www.ngo-marg.org/
- https://www.mdraonline.com/
- https://www.cmie.com/
- https://www.ncaer.org/
- http://nirdpr.org.in/
- http://www.nihfw.org/
- https://cess.ac.in/

- https://www.nilem.com/
- https://iica.nic.in/
- https://adrindia.org/
- https://www.asercentre.org/
- https://en.wikipedia.org/wiki/National_Family_Health_Survey
- https://www.csds.in/
- https://csdindia.org/
- https://cprindia.org/
- https://www.cseindia.org/
- https://www.pacindia.org/
- https://graam.org.in/
- https://www.cmsindia.org/
- *India Today*, December 26, 2022, https://www.indiatoday.in/magazine/editor-s-note/story/20221226-from-the-editor-in-chief-2309690-2022-12-17

Chapter 7

- https://assets.publishing.service.gov.uk/media/57a08abee5274a31e0000754/60911-MappingReport_social_science.pdf
- https://www.financialexpress.com/education-2/23-iits-to-participate-in-iinventiv-mega-fair-to-showcase-research-development-projects/2692537/
- https://www.primepost.in/thanks-to-nep-for-including-research-as-a-concern/
- https://www.news9live.com/knowledge/what-are-ugcs-new-regulations-for-awarding-phd-all-you-need-to-know- about-it-208042
- *The Hindu*, Feb 23, 2022, https://www.thehindu.com/sci-tech/health/methodology-of-csds-lokniti-health-survey/article66542046.ece